Christian Theology

Zondervan Quick-Reference Library

ZONDERVAN
QUICK
REFERENCE
LIBRARY

Christian Theology

John H. Sailhamer

ZondervanPublishingHouse

Grand Rapids, Michigan

A Division of HarperCollinsPublishers

Christian Theology
Copyright © 1998 by John H. Sailhamer

Requests for information should be addressed to:

▦ ZondervanPublishingHouse
Grand Rapids, Michigan 49530

Library of Congress Cataloging-in-Publication Data

Sailhamer, John.
   Christian theology / John H. Sailhamer.
      p. cm. — (Zondervan quick reference library)
   ISBN: 0-310-50041-9
   1. Theology, Doctrinal. I. Title. II. Series.
BT77.S25 1998
230–dc21   97-45990
                                                      CIP

Interior design by Sue Vandenberg Koppenol

Printed in the United States of America

---

98 99 00 01 02 03 04 /❖ DC/ 10 9 8 7 6 5 4 3 2 1

Contents

Abbreviations of the Books of the Bible

Genesis	Gen.	Nahum	Nah.
Exodus	Ex.	Habakkuk	Hab.
Leviticus	Lev.	Zephaniah	Zeph.
Numbers	Num.	Haggai	Hag.
Deuteronomy	Deut.	Zechariah	Zech.
Joshua	Josh.	Malachi	Mal.
Judges	Judg.	Matthew	Matt.
Ruth	Ruth	Mark	Mark
1 Samuel	1 Sam.	Luke	Luke
2 Samuel	2 Sam.	John	John
1 Kings	1 Kings	Acts	Acts
2 Kings	2 Kings	Romans	Rom.
1 Chronicles	1 Chron.	1 Corinthians	1 Cor.
2 Chronicles	2 Chron.	2 Corinthians	2 Cor.
Ezra	Ezra	Galatians	Gal.
Nehemiah	Neh.	Ephesians	Eph.
Esther	Est.	Philippians	Phil.
Job	Job	Colossians	Col.
Psalms	Ps(s).	1 Thessalonians	1 Thess.
Proverbs	Prov.	2 Thessalonians	2 Thess.
Ecclesiastes	Eccl.	1 Timothy	1 Tim.
Song of Songs	Song	2 Timothy	2 Tim.
Isaiah	Isa.	Titus	Titus
Jeremiah	Jer.	Philemon	Philem.
Lamentations	Lam.	Hebrews	Heb.
Ezekiel	Ezek.	James	James
Daniel	Dan.	1 Peter	1 Peter
Hosea	Hos.	2 Peter	2 Peter
Joel	Joel	1 John	1 John
Amos	Amos	2 John	2 John
Obadiah	Obad.	3 John	3 John
Jonah	Jonah	Jude	Jude
Micah	Mic.	Revelation	Rev.

Introduction

What Is This Book?

This book is a new and unique reference tool. Simply put, it is a complete and succinct description of each major Christian teaching that you can read in one minute, only a fraction of the time it takes to use a traditional book of doctrine. You do not need to wade through a lot of information, for this book goes right to the point—the description of the doctrine itself. This book not only takes into account the latest in biblical scholarship, it also shows the sense and place each teaching occupies within the larger structure of Christian doctrine.

Because we get so much of our information in daily life quickly and efficiently, we are becoming increasingly accustomed to having information or knowledge about Christianity given to us in the same way. Though the need for fast delivery systems often undercuts the role of thoughtful reflection in our society, our habits have changed. We have adjusted to the routines of everyday life around us. There is therefore a legitimate need for a more efficient way to build our knowledge of Christian theology—if only as a starting point for more in-depth and reflective understanding.

A regular use of the *Zondervan Quick-Reference Library: Christian Theology* should lead to a more in-depth and knowledgeable study of God's Word. It can, of course, be used along with traditional books on Christian doctrine, and this book is not intended to replace them. Rather, our aim is to supply the legitimate need (or appetite) for efficiency in obtaining Christian knowledge. It is a convenient starting point.

The Study of Theology

A Description of Christian Theology

If we look at the word *theology* and break it down into the two Greek words from which it is composed—*theos* (meaning "God") and *logos* (meaning "study")—theology is "the study of God." In the ancient pagan world, those who knew much about the ancient gods were called *theologians*. This word was simply taken over by the Christian church and used to describe Christian scholars and saints who thought and wrote about God. In that sense even the authors of the Bible were theologians, and what they wrote was theology. In fact, nearly any Christian is a theologian of sorts, and what each thinks about God is his or her theology. Even God is a theologian in that he certainly has thoughts about himself. So are the angels, because they think about God. One can easily see that there can be many kinds of theology.

Strictly speaking, theology is a knowledge of God and divine things. We should add, however, that a theologian not only knows about God, a theologian also knows God. Theology is not a mere set of facts about God; it is a knowledge of God that grows out of a relationship with him. That relationship, for Christian theology, comes through God's Word—both the written Word, the Bible, and the living Word, Jesus Christ. There is a place for knowing God through his works, such as the created world, but the Bible, the Word of God, is the foundation of all Christian theology and the rule of faith.

When it comes to giving expression to our knowledge of God, theology must be personally thought out and written down so that our thoughts about him do not become confused. Theology thus takes on a certain formal character. Some Christians are better at expressing their ideas and organizing their thoughts than others. Over the centuries this has led to a focus of Christian theology on certain key, gifted individuals. There are, in other words, definitive works of theology.

One key purpose for writing out all that one knows about God from Scripture is as a safeguard against erroneous and defective views. The history of Christian theology is, in fact, a history of fending off erroneous, nonbiblical notions about God. Open discussions of theology have thus led to the formation of creeds, that is, succinct statements of theology. The creeds safeguard biblical statements about God from erroneous interpretations. In a sense, we could do without theology and creeds if the Bible were never misunderstood. But we are human, and there is always the chance that people will misunderstand what the Bible teaches about God. There remains, then, an important place for theology in the church and in our lives today.

Natural and Supernatural Theology

What can be known about God apart from Scripture? The answer to that question is the concern of *natural* theology. Paul says (Rom. 2:14–15) that the Gentiles—that is, those who do not have the Scriptures—have the "requirements of the law" written on their heart. That is, they have a human conscience as a source for knowing God's will. Paul also suggests that by observing the world around us we can gain some knowledge about God (1:19–20; cf. Acts 17:27). The Psalms teach that God's glory is revealed in the heavens he created (Ps. 19:1).

What can we know from natural theology? The Bible suggests that the world around us teaches us that there is a God and that he is to be worshiped as the Supreme Being. Moreover, we can conclude from our own conscience that we ought to do what is right and avoid what is wrong. From the fact that we are persons we can conclude that God, our Creator, is personal.

But does such a theology, derived only from nature, provide sufficient knowledge of God to lead us to him and enable us to establish a relationship with him? Can we know God—not just about God—apart from the Scripture? On that question the Bible is quite clear. Peter says about Jesus, for example, "Salvation is found in no one else, for there is no other name under heaven given to men by which we must be saved" (Acts 4:12). About those who did not know the name of Jesus in the past and lived in idolatry, the Bible says, "God overlooked such ignorance," and then adds, "but now he commands all people everywhere to repent" (17:30). There is thus little hope for those who have not heard about or those who reject the name of Jesus. Natural theology does not lead to salvation and fellowship with God.

But God has revealed himself and his will in the Bible, his written Word. Since he has taken the initiative and has made himself known to us in his Word, we can speak of it as a *supernatural* revelation. Thus, alongside a natural theology, there is a supernatural theology, whose goal is to reveal what is necessary for our salvation and how we ought to live.

God had several purposes in giving humanity a written Word. (1) As a written text, he makes the Bible available to everyone. Everyone knows at least one language, and the Bible is understandable as a language. Translations are, of course, necessary because of the multiplicity of languages, and not everyone can read. But the Bible can be read aloud, and people can listen to it. (2) Being committed to writing helps preserve the Bible from damage and corruption over the years. Though mistakes did occur in copying the Bible manuscripts, remarkably accurate copies of the original Bible are available. (3) Most important, we can study and meditate on God's Word throughout the course of everyday life (cf. Ps. 1).

Scripture

The Written Scriptures

God is the one whom we study in theology, and the Bible is the means by which we come to know him. Though some stress the importance of a visionary divine encounter with God, we must not overlook the basic truth that Christianity is a religion of the Bible. We know God as he has revealed himself in his Word. "Like newborn babies," we are to "crave pure spiritual milk" from God's Word (1 Peter 1:25–2:2). "How can a young man keep his way pure?" asks the psalmist; "by living according to your word," is his reply (Ps. 119:9). There is, of course, a subjective side to our knowing God through his Word (cf. 42:2; 84:2); but the important point is that our walk with the Lord and our personal relationship with him develop as we learn of him through his Word. Through the Scriptures we have hope (see Rom. 15:4).

The church itself is built on the foundation of the written Scriptures (Eph. 2:20). They are the norm by which all the beliefs and actions are to be judged (cf. Isa. 8:20). They are "a light shining in a dark place" (2 Peter 1:19). Having insufficient knowledge of Scripture can lead to error (Matt. 22:29). All Christians, even those who are mature and spiritual, are to be subject to the teachings of Scripture (1 Cor. 10:15; Phil. 3:15; 1 John 2:13–14).

The three principle attributes of Scripture are its authority, its perfection, and its clarity. (1) The *authority* of Scripture consists of its claim that we must believe it and obey it as the will of God. The Scriptures do not derive their authority from the church; rather, the church derives its authority from the Scriptures. Ultimately the authority of Scripture is derived from Jesus Christ. The Bible alone is the primary witness to him, and Jesus himself accepted the final authority of the Scriptures (e.g., Matt. 5:17–18; John 17:17).

(2) The *perfection* of Scripture consists of its complete sufficiency for our salvation and godly living. The Bible does not contain the sum total of all knowledge, but it does contain the sum total of all that is necessary to know for our relationship with God (2 Tim. 3:16–17).

(3) The *clarity* of Scripture lies in the fact that what we need to know from the Bible can, in fact, be known simply by reading it. The Bible is not a book of mysteries; it is not impossible to understand. What it has to say, it says clearly to all who read and study it. True, some parts are more difficult than others, and Bible teachers and scholars are needed to sound its depths. But what they teach about the necessary truths of the Bible should be clear to any reader of the Bible.

What Is the Bible?

The Bible is one book made up of many books. These were written over many centuries by authors with vastly different backgrounds and cultures. Many authors are well known: Moses, David, Solomon, Ezra, Paul. Such men are not only the leading characters in the Bible, they are also its leading producers. A surprisingly large number of the biblical authors, however, are nameless. Who wrote 1 and 2 Kings, for example, or the book of Hebrews?

Fortunately, the answer to questions of this nature is of no major consequence in understanding the Bible. Who doesn't know and appreciate an old Hollywood movie from the 30s and 40s? Yet how many know about Irving Thalberg of MGM or Jack Warner of Warner Brothers Studios? These were the men who made or produced the movies; they were the "authors" of those films. But we know the movies by watching them, not by learning about their authors and producers. Similarly, we know the Bible and the books of the Bible by reading them.

Some kinds of books (e.g., a diary) require some information about its author before it can be properly understood. Other books, like works of literature and history, are written so that you don't have to know the author to understand and appreciate them. What you need to know is given to you as you read the text. The Bible is that way: It is written simply to be read.

This may sound obvious, but many biblical scholars disagree. The Bible is often approached today as a book so different from other books and so distant from our world that we need to learn all about its world before we can understand what it says. Though there is some merit to that process, it ignores the fact that the Bible was written with a general audience in mind. Their authors were sensitive to the limitations of time and culture that future readers might encounter. They thus took these limitations into consideration when they wrote their books.

If there was a particular historical or cultural item they felt needed explanation, they did so (see 1 Sam. 9:9). What they didn't feel needed explaining was general knowledge (like what the moon is) or unimportant items (like the color of Sarah's eyes). For the most part, they allow the readers to fill in the blanks of their stories. We, of course, often fall back on popular conceptualizations. But whether Moses looks like Charlton Heston in DeMille's *The Ten Commandments* or Michelangelo's Moses does not affect our understanding of Exodus.

The Bible Is the Word of God

Although the Bible shares features with many other kinds of books, it is a unique book. It is the Word of God. We should say something here about what this statement means. Basically it means two things: (1) The Bible is divine revelation, and (2) the Bible is divinely inspired.

The Bible teaches that God has left signs of his existence and power in his work of creation. From the world around us and from within our own selves we can see evidences of God's glory. For example, from the world around us we see that he is a powerful and wonderful God; from within our own consciences, that he is a personal and holy God. But there is a limit to what can be known about God in that way. Apart from the Bible, for example, we cannot know God's will or God's love for us. We may know from within ourselves that we need God's grace and mercy, but without God's personal speaking to us we cannot know how to receive it. In the Bible God has made known his will for us.

But how does God speak to us in the Bible? It does so like any other book—with letters, words, sentences, and paragraphs. The Bible is a written text. If we can read, we can read the Bible. This all sounds elementary, but it is important. Sometimes the idea is cast about that the Bible is nothing more than human thoughts and aspirations about God. The Christian idea of revelation is much more than that. The Bible may be human words, but those words express the very words that God wants us to know.

How can human words express God's will? The answer to that question leads to the notion of *inspiration*. The books of the Bible were written by human beings who were "carried along" in their writing by the Holy Spirit (2 Peter 1:21), but the Bible never gets more specific than that. It does not tell us *how* the Holy Spirit moved these writers to express God's will. We can safely say that God did not dictate the words of the Bible to the writers, nor did he merely give them suggestions on what to write. In the clear statement of Scripture, its written words are "God-breathed" (2 Tim. 3:16). What the human writers wrote, God intended to say to us.

There are two important implications of the inspiration of Scripture: (1) inerrancy, and (2) the canon.

The Inerrancy of Scripture

When the Bible speaks of its own inspiration (2 Tim. 3:16), it focuses on the final product, the Scriptures, rather than on the process that produced them, namely, the authorship of the Scriptures. We know, of course, that the authors of Scriptures were human beings—godly, but still human. As such they were fully capable of error, both in fact and opinion. The idea of divine inspiration implies that the writers of Scripture were kept from error when they wrote. The Spirit of God moved them to write and supervised their work so that the Scriptures were kept from error. The inerrancy of Scripture is thus part and parcel of the biblical notion of inspiration.

The concept of inerrancy is usually directed at two levels: (1) the subject matter of the biblical books, and (2) the actual words used to describe and discuss the content. Since the Bible is inspired both in its subject matter and words, the notion of inerrancy applies to both. That is, the biblical writers were not only kept from error in recording facts and ideas, but also in their very choice of words. This notion of inerrancy is apparent in the concept of inspiration presented in 2 Timothy 3:16, "All Scripture is God-breathed" ("inspired"). The word "Scripture" in Greek means "the writings." The focus, in other words, is on the written texts. Thus, to say "all the writings" or "all the written texts" are inspired implies both the facts and ideas contained in them and the very words of Scripture as well. This is known as "verbal inspiration."

The notion that "all" the words are inspired is called "verbal *plenary* inspiration" ("plenary" means "all"). A classic statement of such inspiration is that of Jesus in Matthew 5:18: "Until heaven and earth disappear, not the smallest letter, not the least stroke of a pen, will by any means disappear from the Law." Jesus speaks here as if every letter of every word is inspired and irreplaceable.

With such careful attention paid to each letter and each word of Scripture, the natural question is whether the exact words of the inspired authors have been preserved for us today. Do we have exact copies of the original inspired books of the Bible? What about errors by those who hand-copied the Bible for centuries? Fortunately we have many early and well-preserved manuscripts of the Bible. While we do not have the original manuscripts for any book of the Bible, these early copies do give us a remarkably accurate picture of the originals. These early copies also demonstrate how carefully the copyists were as they did their work.

The Canon of Scripture

It is one thing to talk about the Bible in general terms, but just exactly what Bible are we talking about? Isn't there some disagreement on what books are even in the Bible? The answer, of course, is that there is disagreement, but not as much as one might think. The standard for what books are in the Bible and what books are not is called the *canon*.

For the Old Testament, the standard was determined long before the birth of Jesus. We have little direct knowledge of the process that brought this about, but we can say with certainty that the Old Testament we have today is the same Scriptures that Jesus used. It was the accepted standard of the Jews in the first century.

In some parts of the church, in the early centuries A.D., additional books were put alongside the canon of the Old Testament in some manuscripts of the Bible. These were popular works that were used in worship and devotion. Later on some of these works were accepted as part of the canon by the Roman Catholic Church and some Orthodox Churches, though not having the same authority as the Bible. These books (up to eighteen) are called the Apocrypha.

There is no dispute about the canon of the New Testament. At an early stage in the history of the church, the New Testament canon was closed, and no new books were added.

The basis for including a book in the canon of the Old and New Testament was twofold: (1) universal acceptance among God's people—Israel for the Old Testament and the church for the New Testament; (2) internal witness of the Holy Spirit—the Spirit of God bore witness to the early readers of Scripture that these books and no others were the inspired Word of God.

How do we know the early church accepted the right books and genuinely witnessed the Spirit's confirmation? For the Old Testament we have the confirmation of Jesus. Throughout his ministry, Jesus quoted and used the Scriptures as God's Word. To accept his authority is to accept the authority of the Old Testament. For the New Testament we have the confirmation of the apostles—the authoritative men who had received direct instruction from Jesus during his earthly ministry. Their acceptance and confirmation of the canon of the New Testament assures us of its authority in our lives today.

What Is the Old Testament?

The Old Testament is also the Bible of Judaism, where it is called simply the "Hebrew Bible." To speak of an "Old" Testament acknowledges the existence of a "New" Testament. Unfortunately, calling it the "Old" Testament also may imply it has been superseded by the New Testament. That is not the case. The New Testament itself and the Christian church acknowledge the full authority of the Old Testament for the Christian life. By means of these Scriptures, Paul says, the Christian "may be thoroughly equipped for every good work" (2 Tim. 3:17).

Christianity shares the Old Testament with Judaism because Jesus was a Jew and because he saw the whole of his life as a fulfillment of the ancient Jewish prophets' hope in the coming Messiah. Christians believe Jesus is the Messiah long expected by the Old Testament prophets. The Old Testament is thus the basis of the New Testament. Without it the New Testament has little meaning. When John the Baptist, for example, saw Jesus, he said, "Look, the Lamb of God, who takes away the sin of the world" (John 1:29). Without the Old Testament notion of the sacrificial Passover lamb (Ex. 12:23) and the prophet Isaiah's messianic Servant of the Lord who was to give his life as a ransom for sin (Isa. 53:6), John's words cannot be understood.

Long before the birth of Jesus, Jews reverenced and searched their Hebrew Scriptures. They had a deep and sincere hope regarding God's faithfulness to his Word. God, for example, had promised David that a royal son would be born to his house who would rule in peace over Israel and all the nations (2 Sam. 7). Those who wrote the Old Testament had as one of their primary goals the preservation of that hope for generations to come.

Those who collected and preserved the various books of the Old Testament and grouped them into their present form were also motivated by an intense expectation of the coming Savior. The scribe Ezra had much to do with that process (e.g., Ezra 7:10). During his time, the greatest part of the work of collecting and shaping the books of the Old Testament occurred.

An ideal picture of the faithful Jew awaiting the fulfillment of the Old Testament promises can be seen in the old man Simeon, who waited at the temple "for the consolation of Israel" and who immediately recognized Jesus as the promised Savior (Luke 2:25–32).

What Is the New Testament?

The New Testament is the authoritative collection of God-breathed writings. Its books were written by the disciples of Jesus, the apostles, and its main teaching is that the Old Testament promise of the "new covenant [or testament]" (Jer. 31:31) was fulfilled in the death and resurrection of Jesus (Luke 22:20; 2 Cor. 3:6).

The New Testament is shaped around a fourfold purpose. (1) Its initial purpose is to present, in narrative form, the birth, life, death, and resurrection of Jesus Christ. The four "Gospels" each describe events in the life of Jesus. They cite specific messianic prophecies that show how Jesus' life and death fulfilled Old Testament promises.

(2) The rejection of Jesus by the people of Israel, the Jews of his own day, meant that the kingdom promised in the Old Testament would not be established exactly as foretold. But what did happen? What is the church's relationship to the Old Testament promises of the kingdom? To answer these questions the book of Acts was written. Acts explains how a fundamentally Jewish remnant of believers in Jerusalem became, in a short time, a primarily Gentile church, spread throughout the ancient world.

(3) The letters of Paul and the other apostles are devoted to the establishment and development of the Gentile churches. These letters were intended to establish guidelines and basic norms for all churches. They become increasingly concerned about doctrine and the problem of false teachers.

(4) The New Testament concludes by focusing on the return of Christ to establish his kingdom on earth (Revelation).

We learn something about the books of the New Testament by noting how they are arranged. The Gospels provide the basis of all the teaching that follows. Matthew, the most comprehensive, comes first, followed by Mark, a kind of summary. John is inserted between Luke and its sequel, Acts, perhaps because of John's emphasis on the Holy Spirit. In Acts 28 Paul is in Rome, preaching the gospel. This book is then followed by his letter to the Roman church, and then by the rest of his letters. Then comes Hebrews, which explains the deeper matters of the gospel. The general letters and Revelation close the New Testament.

The Being of God

Who Is God?

It is difficult to decide where to start in a discussion about God. The usual starting point is the question: Is there a God? Before we can answer that question, however, we must ask what God are we talking about? Even to ask the question about the existence of God means we have some idea of who or what God we are talking about. Thus we find that we must assume something about the nature of God even before we can determine whether or not he exists. But if we assume something about God, will that not determine the answer to this question? We seem caught in a circle. To think our way out of this dilemma, we must start with a general description of who or what God is. We will call this our working definition.

Our starting point is to define God as an independent being who governs all and on which all else depends. What we are really asking, then, is whether there is "an independent being who governs all and on which all else depends." Note that we are not here talking about the God who has revealed himself in the Bible. Are there reasonable grounds for saying that "an independent being who governs all and on which all else depends" exists?

The belief that such a being does in fact exist is called Theism. The belief that denies the existence of such a being is called Atheism. The term Atheism, of course, stands not only for the denial of the existence of the God we have described above (Theism), but also for the denial that any kind of God or gods exist. It is difficult to maintain a truly atheistic position, for how can one prove that something does not exist? The best an atheist can hope for is to prove that belief in God is unreasonable or self-contradictory. But neither of these points can be easily maintained. There is nothing contradictory in believing that God exists and, as we shall see, it certainly is not unreasonable. Most atheists admit this and prefer to hold to the position called Agnosticism.

Agnosticism is the belief that we cannot know with reasonable certainty whether there is a God. There may be evidence that God exists, but, the agnostic maintains, there is simply not enough evidence to provide sufficient grounds for faith. But how much evidence is needed to provide "sufficient grounds" for faith? In actual fact we cannot demand a certain amount of evidence. We have to weigh what evidence we have. Our decision must be based on the available evidence, rather than on what evidence we may wish to have. The theistic arguments for the existence of God (see next unit) are thus of great importance to Christian theology. They show that the available evidence supports the Christian view of God.

Arguments for the Existence of God

Our goal in the following arguments for the existence of God is simply to demonstrate that there is reasonable evidence to support faith in God. We are not attempting to prove God's existence, but to look at the world around us and at ourselves and ask whether there are sufficient grounds for believing in "an independent being who governs all and on which all else depends."

(1) *The argument from causes.* When something happens in everyday experience, we look for a cause. If our car stalled on a busy expressway, it would not be reasonable to say, "It just happened." We want to know the cause of the engine failure or to find someone who knows what the trouble is. Our whole life is full of causes and effects. In the same way, when we look at the universe around us, it is unreasonable to say, "It just happened." It is reasonable to look for a cause to the universe, that is, "an independent being on which all else depends."

(2) *The argument from design.* If we see something around us that has an intricate design, such as a computer, we naturally understand that someone has designed it. It is absurd to think that such a device "just happened." The universe is far more complex than a computer, and it is unreasonable to believe it "just happened." Like the computer, the universe most likely had a designer, a Creator.

(3) *The argument from human nature.* We as human beings know ourselves as thinking, feeling, and acting persons. We remember the past and have hopes for the future. Through all of our experiences we retain our own identity. It is reasonable to believe that such knowledge of ourselves is real, not just an illusion. If so, then it is also reasonable to believe that we as persons owe our existence to another, similar person—that is, to God—and not to mere blind chance.

(4) *The argument from morality.* Certain values are basic to human nature. As human beings we have an innate sense of right and wrong, fairness, justice, freedom. and responsibility. We experience guilt when we have done wrong and indignation when we have been wronged. It is reasonable to believe that behind such human values lies a higher standard of divine values.

(5) *The argument from human reason.* Ultimately, the use of our reasoning abilities depends on our thoughts fitting together and making sense. That is, in fact, what we call being reasonable. When we apply those reasoning abilities to the question of God's existence, we find that we can easily think of a Supreme Being, far greater than ourselves and the world. The existence of God makes sense, at least to our minds. This may not prove that God exists, but it does confirm that the existence of God is a reasonable idea.

The Essence of God: What Is God?

There is a difference between the question, What is God? and the question, Who is God? It is similar to the difference between the question, What is a human being? and, Who is George Washington? When we ask, What is God? or, What is a human being? we are asking about the essential nature of God or a human being. What defines them? In the case of human beings, we have many examples from which to draw a general description of what makes up a human being. Thus when we ask, Who is George Washington? we already know what a human being is.

In the case of God, however, we have only one example, God himself. The question, What is God? therefore, sounds somewhat redundant. The simple answer is that God is God. It is incorrect to say God is a god. To say "a god" implies that there is a general category of which God is a specific example. There is, however, no general category with God. There is only one example—God himself. When we speak of the essence of God—that is, what makes God to be what he is—we are speaking of something that is one of a kind.

Therefore, we must be careful how we use language in describing God. The words we use, of course, come from the language we use in everyday life. But when we use such words to speak about God, we must remember we are using them in a unique way. That is, when we use "goodness," "love," and "mercy" to refer to God, we know what these words mean from our own experience. We have a sense of what "goodness" is because we have known good people and enjoyed good things. But when we use these words to speak about God, we mean them in a full and perfect sense. To say God is good means he is absolutely good. When used of God, then, "good" means something like it does in ordinary language; but in actual fact it has a unique meaning— "perfectly good."

Sometimes when we speak about God, we have to use words that have no real meaning in our own experience. We have an inkling what these words mean, but we do not know it from experience. We can say, for example, that God is "infinite," though no human being knows from experience what it means to be "infinite." We as "finite" creatures know what it means to be "finite," but what does it mean to be "infinite"? We don't really know. All we can say is God is "not finite like us." The same thing can be said about many of the unique attributes of God.

Incommunicable Attributes of God

An *attribute* of God is a perfect quality or characteristic that makes him who he is. His attributes characterize him alone. It is because these qualities truly describe him that he is God. An attribute is *incommunicable* when it is true *in any sense* only of God; there are no analogies to human qualities or character. God's attributes describe his inner essence. Thus, when we say God is infinite and God is wise, we mean not just that God is infinite and also wise, but that God is infinitely wise. What is true about any one attribute is true about all the rest.

Spirituality. God has no material body. He does not have flesh and bones. For human beings, who are essentially physical, it is impossible to conceive of existence without some material component. In the languages of the Bible (Hebrew and Greek), the word "spirit" means "wind." The writers chose that word to describe God because it most clearly expresses the notion of immateriality (John 3:6–8; 4:24). Thus, when the Bible speaks of the hands or eyes of God, it is only speaking about God figuratively.

Unity. There is only one God. He alone is God; there is none beside him (Isa. 44:8). Human beings, as individuals, have a unity in themselves. But they can also exist alongside other human beings. One human being is not exclusive of another human being. God's unity, however, is exclusive. There can be no other God beside him.

Eternality. God has no beginning and will have no end (Ps. 102:25–27). Moreover, there is no succession of time in his own personal existence. That does not mean, however, that he is ignorant of time. He knows of every moment of time because, since the first moment, he has existed as eternally present. We cannot think of human existence in this way. God, however, is not limited to time.

Independence. God does not owe his existence or his nature to anyone or anything. Human beings and all creation, however, are totally dependent on him.

Infinity. There are no limits to God's existence. He is perfect. By comparison, our own human existence is finite; we are limited to time and space.

Immutability. God does not change (Ps. 102:27). Both in essence (that is, who he is) and in his will (that is, what he intends to do), God remains the same. Since God is perfect, change would necessarily mean to become less than he is—less than perfect. That cannot be!

Simplicity. Though the material world is composed of various fragments and the human mind cannot function without dividing its object of thought into logical segments, God's essence cannot be so divided. Though God has three persons, he has only one, simple essence.

Communicable Attributes of God

A *communicable* attribute is one in which its qualities and characteristics are true not only of God but in an analogous sense also of human beings. As divine attributes, they are true of God in a perfect and absolute sense.

God's will. God desires certain things and not others. He intends to accomplish certain goals and not others. He requires certain actions and not others. These are all expressions of his will. God's will can be exercised in a *determinative* sense, in which he causes something to be or to happen (Eph. 1:11); in a *permissive* sense, in which he allows something to occur (Acts 2:23); and in a *prescriptive* sense, in which he expresses his desire for response from his creatures: "Teach me to do your will, for you are my God" (Ps. 143:10).

God's power. Human beings have a will, but they are not always able to accomplish what they desire. God, however, is always able to accomplish what he wills (Ps. 115:3). He does so perfectly because he is all-powerful (Rev. 1:8).

God's justice. God is totally without any fault. He always acts according to his own standard of perfection, for he is just and holy. In his response to human actions he punishes sin and disobedience and rewards faithfulness and obedience.

God's goodness. God is the highest good: "How great is your goodness" (Ps. 31:19). He always acts beneficially toward all his creation (Acts 14:17), especially his own people (Ps. 73:1).

God's love. God's love consists of his acts of goodness on behalf of his creatures. He loved the world before he created it (John 3:16); and even after his creation rebelled against him and sought to find their own good apart from him, he still loved them and provided for their salvation (Eph. 5:25). God's love for his creatures extends throughout all eternity.

God's grace. God's unmerited love for fallen humanity is the expression of his grace. The basis of his grace is, and always has been, the work of Christ in bearing the punishment for our sin. There is nothing humanity can do to earn God's love and goodness. Jesus paid it all.

God's mercy. God's response to the pitiful human condition, the effect of humanity's own rebellion from God, is a desire to help and give comfort. That expression of his will is mercy.

God's dominion. God has the last word, "He is the LORD; let him do what is good in his eyes" (1 Sam. 3:18). He is not answerable to anyone, but all are answerable to him (Acts 17:25).

God's Knowledge

God's knowledge is different from ours. For example, he knows all things perfectly—the past, the present, and the future. He also knows himself. Moreover, God knows all things in their essence; that is, he does not have to perceive them as we humans do, through our senses. Thus for God, knowledge and understanding are the same.

We do not have a difficult time understanding how God can know the *past*. He is eternal and thus has been eternally present to each moment in the past. His knowledge of the past is analogous to our memory, through which we can relive the past. God's knowledge of the *present* is similar to our knowledge of the world, which is limited to our senses of sight, sound, smell, taste, and hearing. We have some understanding of what it means for God to have knowledge of the present. But when it comes to God's knowledge of the *future*, we cannot understand it fully. Thus opinions differ widely on the exact nature of God's knowledge of the future.

Everyone agrees the Bible teaches that God knows the future. Whatever happens, God knows all about it and knew all about it from eternity past. But what about those human acts and decisions that rely on free will? Does God know with certainty, from eternity past, what men and women will do and think of their own free will? Or does the fact that God knows with certainty everything that happens leave no room for human free will?

Most answers to this question end up either limiting human free will or limiting the extent of God's knowledge. (1) If God really knows the future with certainty, then he must know what human beings will do of their own free will. If God knows what those choices will be, then is not our free will determined by that knowledge? The certainty of God's knowledge alone makes the outcome of our free will just as certain. How could we do or decide differently than what God already knows? (2) If, on the other hand, we say that our free will is not determined by God's knowledge, then God's knowledge is less than certain. If we are truly free to choose, how can he know for certain what our choice will be? He may know what we would probably do, but he could not know for certain what we would chose. It seems that the choice is left up to us at the moment of the decision and God's knowledge is subject to revision based on our decision.

Perhaps the best way to express it is to say that God's knowledge of the future is a knowledge of what we will, in fact, choose to do. In his foreknowledge, God already knows what we will freely choose in the course of time.

The Trinity

There is one God, who exists in three persons. Human beings exist as persons. Each one is a unique and distinct person. Moreover, each human person shares a common human nature. There are thus many persons, but only one human nature. Each person is united to that human nature—but who can explain how? It is a mystery. We have to invent words to describe our participation in the human essence, though we all know what that is. Is it any surprise that when we try to understand the personhood of God we also face a fundamental mystery?

From simple observation of ourselves and others we see two basic laws that govern the essential makeup of human beings. (1) Human nature is divisible. Each person has his or her own share of human nature; that share has been called a subsistence. (2) Two or more persons cannot share the same subsistence. Human persons, therefore, "subsist" (that is, exist) as "unities."

When we attempt to understand the biblical view of the Triune God, we must be careful not to impose on him the laws that govern the makeup of human beings. The two basic laws of human nature mentioned above are not true of God. (1) God's nature or essence is unique. There is only one divine nature, and it is not divisible like human nature. (2) Unlike the "unity" of subsistence of human persons, in God three divine persons share a single subsistence. The one God "subsists" (that is, exists) in three persons. That is the notion of the Trinity.

The concept of the Trinity is difficult to understand because there are no analogies in human experience. Any apparent analogies fall short of explanation and often lead to more misunderstanding. We can better grasp the concept if we acknowledge from the start that God is not like us. There is only one of him, hence there is only one divine nature; yet the three divine persons—the Father, the Son, and the Holy Spirit (Matt. 28:19)—share the same essence. But how three persons can "subsist" in one essence is no greater mystery than how one person can "subsist" in one essence. The fact that we, as human beings, accept without question the concept of one person subsisting in one essence blinds us to the mystery of that "unity." Recognizing that mystery opens us to the greater mystery of the divine "Trinity." The Trinity does not mean there are three Gods (Tritheism). Nor does the Trinity appear as one God as three successive persons (Modalism). Rather, three distinct, eternally existing persons exist in one divine nature.

The Persons of the Trinity

The identity of the three divine persons in the Trinity—the Father, the Son, and the Holy Spirit—grows out of the eternal relationship between them, our knowledge of which comes directly from the Bible. Jesus commissioned the disciples to proclaim the gospel to the nations "in the name of the Father and of the Son and of the Holy Spirit" (Matt. 28:19). In other words, a clear role relationship exists between these three equally divine persons. The Son, for example, asked the Father to send the Holy Spirit to minister to the disciples (John 14:16), and when the Son ascended to the Father, he sent the Holy Spirit to testify concerning himself (John 15:26; Acts 2:33). It is only possible to describe the particular role of each person in a general way.

The Father. The first person of the Trinity is the Father. He is "first" in order, though not first in deity, for the Son and the Spirit are of equal deity with the Father. His role of fatherhood is being the Father of the Son. Though God is our Father (Rom. 8:14–15) and we his children (8:16), this is different from his being the Father of the second person. In that relationship, he is the Father because he has "begotten" (that is, generated) the Son.

The Son. The Bible calls the second person of the Trinity "the Son of God" (Rom. 1:4). He is the "only begotten God" (John 1:18 NASB), the "only begotten from the Father" (1:14 NASB). Because the Son is eternal, the generation of the Son by the Father is not an event at a certain point in time, but is an eternal generation. This was a part of the messianic hope in the Old Testament. The poetic figure of "wisdom" (Prov. 8:12), cast as a craftsman (8:30) working at God's side, speaks of being "appointed" and "given birth" before the beginning of time (8:23, 25). This craftsman is further identified as God's Son (30:4).

The Son is generated by the Father, but not created. He and the Father coexist eternally. It should also be kept in mind that the generation of the Son by the Father does not refer to the birth of Christ in Bethlehem. Jesus Christ was born (John 1:14) into the family of David (Rom. 1:3) at a specific point in time (Luke 2:1–2), but that Son had eternally existed with the Father from all eternity (Mic. 5:2; John 1:1). The Son is the one through whom God made himself known to humanity (John 1:1, 18; Heb. 1:2) and through whom God works. The two great works of God, creation and redemption, are the specific accomplishment of the Son (John 1:3, 17; Heb. 1:3).

The Holy Spirit. Regarding the relationship of the third person of the Trinity to the other two, we know only that he eternally "proceeds" from the Father and the Son (John 15:26).

The Work of God

The Decrees of God

So far we have spoken only of God's essence—that which makes him God. Now we speak of God's actions—what God does as God. Some of God's actions are directed at himself (e.g., the relationship that exists among the persons of the Trinity); other actions are directed at the world, his creation. Of those actions that are directed at the world, some of them are eternal (they were accomplished in God's mind in eternity past), while others are temporal (they are accomplished within the framework of time). One eternal act of God directed to the world is his *divine decree*. In actual fact there is only one divine decree, though one can speak of divine decrees in the plural because, from a human perspective, there are many aspects to God's decree.

What exactly is the divine decree? It is the definite plan in God's mind that establishes from all eternity what is to be or is not to be (Acts 15:18); that decree is not subject to change in any respect. The motive behind God's decree(s) is his free will. His decrees are the fundamental cause of all that God does with respect to his creation and creatures. They are, as it were, the blueprint of his plan for the world. Having been perfectly planned by him in eternity, his decrees are carried out in time. Long before he begins his work, God, like a great artist, has a clear idea of all that he wants to do and make. As the perfect artist, God accomplishes his plan.

God's decrees can be spoken of in three distinct categories. (1) God's *effective* decrees are those that result in any action caused by the decree itself. Jesus Christ, for example, was chosen as the Redeemer "before the creation of the world" (1 Peter 1:20). (2) God's *moral* decrees are what he has mandated or commanded. A moral decree must be enacted by a human being. God, for example, decreed that Israel should obey his commandments. (3) God's *permissive* decrees are those that he allows to happen, though he is not the cause of the action. Christ's death on the cross, for example, was carried out by the Roman government, but it was accomplished according to "God's set purpose and foreknowledge" (Acts 2:23).

The primary focus of a discussion of God's decrees is his plan of salvation. The Bible is clear that not all of humanity will be saved; some will perish and be eternally lost. To what extent does God's decree play a role in determining who will believe in Christ and be saved and who will not? That is the question of predestination.

The Decree of Predestination

In the popular mind, the term *predestination* usually means the decree of God whereby he determined in eternity past the destiny of all of humankind, both the saved and the lost. When somebody says, "You don't believe in predestination, do you?" they usually have that sense in mind. This is an unfortunate use of the term because it overlooks several important qualifications. More precisely, predestination refers *only* to God's decree to save those who believe in Christ. God, in his infinite grace and mercy, has chosen to save some, not all, of humanity. He chose to save those who believe (John 3:16). Theologians have been careful to use the word *predestination* in that precise sense.

But we may still ask, Why didn't God save everyone? Did he predestine to salvation only those whom he knew would believe? Or did his choosing them ensure that they would eventually believe? We cannot answer these questions. We cannot even say why God chose to save anyone—"the depths of the riches of the wisdom and knowledge of God" are unsearchable to us (Rom. 11:33). In the last analysis, the Bible teaches that God's decree to save some, but not all, was determined by his love (Eph. 1:4b), his good pleasure and will (1:5, 9), his own counsel (1:11), and his foreknowledge (Rom. 8:29).

Though this may appear as little more than splitting hairs over the correct terms, it is important to note that the term used to describe God's decree with respect to the lost whom he passes over is *preordination*. God, in eternity past, decreed to "pass by" some of the lost, leaving them to pay the penalty for their own sins, that is, eternal death. God did not preordain them to fall or to be lost, for they were already fallen and lost of their own accord.

In his introduction to the great epic *Paradise Lost*, John Milton states that his purpose was to "justify the ways of God to men." We are not trying to do that here. In all honesty, we are not sure we are capable of that. We are satisfied here if you have a clear picture of the biblical sense of predestination—the act of God's grace that saves those who do not deserve it. But this definition leaves unexplained the question of why God did not decree to save everyone. That is a part of the equation we will never know. We can rest assured, however, that God sees the whole picture and that he has acted according to his infinite wisdom.

Free Will

In speaking of God's decree to predestine some of the lost to eternal salvation, the question of the role of human free will arises. The term *free will* is really redundant. There is only one kind of "will"—a free one. By definition, the notion of a human will includes the concept of freedom. Human beings may be constrained to act or think against their own will, but it is absurd to suggest that they could be constrained "to will" against their own will. Furthermore, the concept of a "human will" is redundant. To have a will is to be human. Not to have a will is to be something other than fully human. We can state emphatically, then, that all human beings have a will and all human wills are free.

Here, then, is where the question arises with the concept of divine predestination. If God elects to save some lost souls and not others, how can it be said that these persons have a say in the matter? Does not God's decree to save some of the lost overrule their free will? Does not this make salvation of the lost little more than an arbitrary divine act about which human beings have little to say? What happens to free will in the course of God's decree?

In response to these questions, we must remember several things. According to the Bible, lost humanity does not will to obtain God's salvation. "There is no one who understands, no one who seeks God" (Rom. 3:11). Why? Because human beings have willfully turned their backs on God (3:12). God did not coerce them to turn away from him; they freely chose to go their own way (cf. Gen. 3). Their will has been depraved (Rom. 1:28–29). As a result, God "gave them over in the sinful desires of their heart" (1:24). In other words, free will does human beings no good when it comes to accepting God's salvation.

God's decree to save the lost, therefore, must include a remedy for our depraved wills. That remedy is the free gift of faith in Christ (Rom. 3:22). God gives faith to the rebellious sinner so he or she can turn to God (Eph. 2:8). Jesus, the Son of God, is "the author and perfecter of our faith" (Heb. 12:2). Without that faith to believe the gospel, humanity's free will only serves to steer them further and further away from God. In a certain sense, then, God's decree to save the lost does, in fact, override humanity's corrupt free will, but it does so in grace (Eph. 2:8).

Are the lost, then, saved against their will? No. God gives them faith and that faith renews their will so that they gladly turn toward the Savior (2 Cor. 4:6).

Creation

We have thus far been speaking of God's actions in terms of his eternal decrees. Other divine actions are not eternal and are carried out in time. Some of them concern the natural world, such as creation and providence; others concern redemption, such as God's sending Christ to die on the cross. Creation is thus an act of God in time by which he brought the world into existence, creating it out of nothing (Heb. 11:3). He "willed" it into existence. Before that act of creation, there was only God—God and nothing, or nobody, else. God, of course, existed as the Triune God in perfect harmony and fellowship. There was no need on his part to create the world. Creation was a pure act of kindness, or grace, toward the world he would create.

The fact that God created the world out of nothing means that, in the Bible's view of things, there is only one ultimate reality—God. The world is not eternal, nor are material things of eternal value. This view of the world and of life in general is contrary to much of modern thinking. As creatures living in a material world, we tend to value ourselves and our world above God. The Bible presents just the opposite. God is the only reality worth our total praise and devotion. Human beings, created in God's image, are given the highest value among all of God's creatures, but they are not God. They are only created "like him" and, as the Bible presents it, they are to live their lives in recognition of their Creator.

In the biblical account of creation we see two aspects of God's work. (1) God's creation of the universe. The expression "the heavens and the earth" means "everything"—the sun, moon, stars, and all the earth (Gen. 1:1). (2) God's preparation of the land. The land was at first uninhabitable (1:2); then God made it a good place for men and women to live in (1:3–31). He is the God who provides a good land for them and cares for them as a loving father.

When did God create the universe? The Hebrew word "beginning" does not refer to a point in time. It refers instead to an indeterminate period of time before the actual reckoning of time begins. Thus, God created the universe before the first week of Genesis 1:2–2:3. During that time, which could have been millions or even billions of years, the universe as we know it today was formed and shaped. Though they are not specifically mentioned, we can assume that it was during this time that prehistoric creatures such as dinosaurs lived and flourished. The fact that some animals and plants were created in "the land" in Genesis 1 does not imply there were no others before that time. In the case of the creation of the man and woman, however, we are told specifically that all humanity finds its origin in them alone (cf. Gen. 2–3).

The Created World

What kind of world did God create? That is one of the chief questions that the biblical writers set out to answer. In their narratives of creation and redemption, they were not merely providing "lessons" in the stories they wrote; their fundamental concern was to depict a world in which those lessons made sense. In fact, they were not so much depicting a world as defining the essential characteristics of all reality.

Most traditional readers of the Bible are familiar with the world represented there. Indeed, it can be argued that until recently the biblical world was the way in which the Western world conceptualized reality. In the world of the Bible, God is an active agent. He is there, and we must reckon with him—or face the consequences. In the account of the Flood (Gen. 6–9), for example, God takes the whole human race to task for their sins, and only a few are saved from judgment. This account serves as a paradigm of the final judgment, in which God will hold all of us accountable. The stories of the cities of Babylon (ch. 11), Sodom and Gomorrah (ch. 19), and the Exodus (Ex. 1–12) reinforce the biblical view that in the real world, God must be taken seriously. The biblical writers challenge us to accept this view of the world as our own.

An important feature of the biblical world in which God is an active agent is the presence of miracles. Unlike the modern world, where miracles are taken as a sign of God's existence, miracles in the Bible are a sign of God's pleasure or displeasure with his creatures. Lot's sons laughed at the idea that God would destroy the city of Sodom (Gen. 19:14). Today they might well laugh at the thought that there is a God at all.

The biblical narratives also present us with a world in which evil is present. Though the world has been created good, evil and rebellion against God have gained a strong foothold in the human heart and manifest themselves in such common social problems as broken homes (Gen. 3:16), murder (4:8), oppression (Ex. 1), and warfare (Gen. 14). This is often a world in which the good suffer and evil grows increasingly more pervasive. But God oversees this world, and his justice will eventually prevail (Gen. 18:25). Finally, the biblical world is one that exhibits clear patterns in the divine activity. When God acts, he does so in ways that foreshadow his future acts. His actions bespeak his character and his plans for the world.

Angels

Angels are an important part of God's world. Though the Bible rarely focuses our attention solely on them, they are present as part of the fabric of the created world. Angels were posted at the entrance to the Garden of Eden to keep fallen humanity from eating of the Tree of Life (Gen. 3:24). Both Abraham and Lot were visited by angels (chs. 18–19), serving as special messengers to announce both blessing (18:10) and judgment (19:12–13). Jacob wrestled with an angel (32:22–32; Hos. 12:4). An angel guided the way of Abraham's servant in his quest for Isaac's wife (Gen. 24:7, 40). An angel accompanied the Israelites through the desert (Ex. 14:19; 32:34). Thousands of angels were with God on Mount Sinai when he gave Israel the Law (Deut. 33:2). The angel Gabriel was sent to Daniel in exile to give him understanding of his prophetic visions (Dan. 8:15–16). Angels ministered to Jesus in the desert, after he had been tempted by the devil (Matt. 4:11). On the eve of Peter's trial before King Herod, an angel appeared in his jail cell and led him in a daring escape (Acts 12:6–10).

In summary, angels are beings who serve as God's special messengers ("angel" means "messenger"). They have no standard appearance. Some appear as ordinary men (Gen. 18:2); others as special apparitions, awesome to look at (Judg. 13:6). At Christ's ascension they were "two men dressed in white" (Acts 1:10). Popular imagery of them as having wings comes from Isaiah's vision of the throne room of heaven, where God was surrounded by "seraphs, each with six wings" (Isa. 6:1–2). It is even possible to entertain "angels without knowing it" (Heb. 13:2).

The Bible suggests there are various kinds and ranks of angels. One is "the angel of the LORD" (Ex. 3:2), which some take to be the preincarnate Christ. The angel Michael is called "the archangel" (Jude 9), and there are "cherubim" (Gen. 3:24) and "seraphs" (Isa. 6:2). Just what the particular roles of each of these kinds of angels are is not explained in the Bible.

Nor does the Bible give an account of the creation of the angels, though they are clearly created beings (Col. 1:16–17). We do not know on which day of the week God created them. What is perhaps most important to note about angels is that, apart from announcing God's acts of salvation (cf. Luke 1–2), their specific roles center on glorifying God (Rev. 5:11–12) and watching over God's people (Matt. 18:10; Heb. 1:14). Some angels sinned and thus fell from their original state of goodness (2 Peter 2:4). These are Satan and his demons.

Satan and Demons

Evil exists in God's good world. That evil came from a single rebellious act of a one-time great angel of God, Lucifer. Jesus said of him, "He was a murderer from the beginning, not holding to the truth" (John 8:44). The book of Revelation identifies him as "that ancient serpent called the devil, or Satan, who leads the whole world astray" (Rev. 12:9). In Jude we are told that some angels "did not keep their positions of authority but abandoned their own home" (Jude 6). From such passages we can reconstruct a general outline about Satan and his demons.

It is clear, first, that Satan and his demons are fallen angels. They were created good along with the rest of God's creation (Gen. 1:31), but they rebelled, lost their standing with God, and are now "spiritual forces of evil in the heavenly realms" (Eph. 6:12). Through them sin and rebellion entered into the human race and the rest of creation, for the serpent (representing "Satan," meaning "adversary") tempted Eve in the Garden of Eden (Gen. 3).

We learn more about the fall of Satan in the prophetic imagery Ezekiel uses to describe the forces of evil in his own day. Ezekiel accuses the king of Tyre of the same sin of pride and arrogance that the angel Lucifer (Satan) displayed in his defiant rebellion from God's rule. Thus, by paying close attention to Ezekiel's imagery (Ezek. 28:11–19), we can catch a glimpse of the events that led to Satan's fall. Originally, Satan was "the model of perfection, full of wisdom and perfect in beauty" (28:12). He lived "in Eden, the garden of God" (28:13), surrounded by the beauty prepared for him when he was created (28:13). He was "blameless in [his] ways" (28:15). All this changed, however, when his "heart became proud on account of [his] beauty" (28:17), and his wisdom was corrupted (28:17).

Isaiah uses similar imagery as he describes the fall of Babylon (Isa. 14:3–23); through it we can add to our picture of the fall of Satan. Satan is the "morning star" (Lucifer), "fallen from heaven" (14:12). He said in his heart, "I will ascend to heaven; I will raise my throne above the stars of God; I will sit enthroned on the mount of assembly. . . . I will make myself like the Most High" (14:13–14). In other words, pride and power lay at the heart of his sin. It is thus no accident that Satan's first temptation of Eve centered on her desire to "be like God" (Gen. 3:5).

The biblical writers take seriously the threat of Satan and his angels. Christians must "put on the full armor of God so that you can take your stand against the devil's schemes" (Eph. 6:11). The devil "prowls around like a roaring lion looking for someone to devour" (1 Peter 5:8); we must resist him by "standing firm in the faith" (5:9).

Creation of Humanity

The central focus of the Bible's account of creation is the story of the origin of the human race. Genesis 1 views humanity "from the top down." The stress falls on the uniqueness of the man and the woman and on their relationship with God. They alone, not the animals, are created in the image of God (Gen. 1:26). They alone, not the animals, have dominion over the rest of God's creation (1:26–28). In a real sense, the world was made for them, and they were made to enjoy fellowship with God.

This view of the importance of humanity is significant for the themes and purpose of the rest of the Bible. Its narratives plot the course of humanity, from the Fall to Redemption, showing that God intended from the beginning to have fellowship with his human creatures. In the Incarnation, God actually became a part of humanity. He sent the Redeemer into the world to save humanity. In doing so, God also redeemed his entire creation back to himself (Rom. 8:21). In the Bible's view of the future, the restoration of all of God's creatures plays an important role. In the new heavens and new earth, "the wolf and the lamb will feed together" (Isa. 65:25).

In contrast to Genesis 1, chapter 2 views the creation of the man and the woman "from the ground up." The man is formed "from the dust of the ground" (2:7), where he shares a common element with the rest of God's creation (cf. the animals also being formed "from the ground"; 2:19). The woman is taken "from the side" (or rib) of the man (2:21–22).

What is the chief end of the human race? The Bible's answer to this question is straightforward: Humanity's chief end is *to worship God* (though our present translations do not make this clear). According to Genesis 2:15, God put the man into the Garden of Eden "to work it and take care of it." We usually understand "it" to refer to the Garden of Eden. That, however, is not likely in the Hebrew text. Another way to read this verse is that God put the man into the garden "for worship and obedience." That is, God's goal in creation was not to populate the world with gardeners but to fill it with worshipers with whom he could have fellowship (cf. Isa. 61:5–6). In the concluding remarks of Genesis 2 we see a further goal of the creation of both the man and the woman: a man will "be united to his wife, and they will become one flesh" (2:24). Marriage is God's purpose for a man and a woman. In that relationship they may fulfill God's blessing to "be fruitful and increase in number; fill the earth and subdue it" (1:28).

God's Providence

God continues to maintain the world he created (Gen. 8:22). His act of governing the world is called *providence*. Not only does God cause the world to follow its own natural laws, but he also watches over it to ensure that everything goes according to his will and his divine decrees (Eph. 1:11). He makes sure that his eternal decrees are accomplished when, where, and how he intended them.

God's providence is universal—not just over the mighty forces of nature (Neh. 9:6) and the great events of history (2 Chron. 36:23), but over even the smallest natural event and the most insignificant human affair (Luke 12:7). God works in "all things" (Rom. 8:28); nothing is too insignificant to merit his attention and care. He makes the grass grow for cattle (Ps. 104:14) and waters the trees for the birds to nest in (104:16–17). All the animals look to him daily for food (104:27). The very lives of God's creatures depend on the breath God gives them. Were he to stop caring for them, they would die (104:29). He has established and maintains the laws for the ordering of day and night (Jer. 33:20). He also determines the course of human history (Prov. 21:1; Acts 17:26), raising up mighty nations and kingdoms (Dan. 2:37) and bringing them to ruin (2:44).

If God's providential care for his creation is so extensive and pervasive, does anything ever happen by accident? Does anything escape his notice or lie outside his concern? No! When an innocent man, for example, accidentally kills another human being, the Bible says that "God lets it happen" (Ex. 21:13). When men throw dice, "its every decision is from the LORD" (Prov. 16:33). Even things with evil intention can accomplish God's intended good (Gen. 50:20).

Is any room left for human decisions? Are our lives totally predetermined by God? No. We as responsible human beings must plan and control our own lives, though we must not forget God's will (Prov. 16:1). We must "commit to the LORD whatever [we] do" (16:3), in order that our plans may succeed. We must say, "If it is the Lord's will, we will live and do this or that" (James 4:15). In other words, God's providence works through our plans and choices. Human beings always and only do what they will to do. Their will is not coerced by God's will. As Joseph told his brothers, "You intended to harm me, but God intended it for good" (Gen. 50:20). Of their own will, his brothers intended their action for harm, but God intended it for good.

Nature

Nature is that part of God's creation that does not have freedom to act as it chooses. In other words, it is all of creation except humanity and angels, who are the only truly free agents in God's created universe. Nature with its processes is the direct product of God's eternal plan. He created nature and now sustains and governs it. The Bible is clear that the whole of nature is dependent on God's will and power.

The term sometimes used to describe the Bible's view of nature is *biblical realism*. The classic statement of this view of nature comes from the philosopher and biblical scholar Saint Augustine (354–430). According to him, the world is the realization of the mind of God. To be "in nature" is to be "in the mind of God." That is, everything we see around us as nature— the birds singing, trees, boulders, lakes, rivers, clouds, stars, etc.—was once a mere thought in God's mind. God conceived, planned, and created all that we now know as nature. When we thus walk through nature, we are, in a real sense, walking through the mind of God.

Such a concept may seem difficult to grasp until you think about being in a place like Disneyland. When you walk through Disneyland, you are, in a real sense, walking through the mind of Walt Disney. At one time Disneyland was only a thought in the planner's mind; Disneyland is the product of his mind. That is how Augustine thought of nature as the realization of the mind of God. Nature and our place in nature were carefully conceived and planned by God long before he brought it into being.

The Bible is also clear that nature is not a part of God himself. It was created out of nothing (Gen. 1:1; Heb. 11:3); it is not eternal. There was a moment when it came into being, there will be a moment when it passes away (2 Peter 3:10), and there will be a moment when it will be restored as a "new heavens and a new earth" (Isa. 65:17).

According to the Bible, God acts in nature, and nature carries out his plan. Nature itself is good (Gen. 1:31), but in the fall of humanity, nature was subjected to the curse (3:17; Rom. 8:20–21). Through nature God reveals his own deity and power to his creatures (Rom. 1:19–20). In the Incarnation, the eternal Son of God entered into and became a part of nature.

History

The Old Testament records historical events that provide the basic framework for the early history of the world. It is precisely that history that leads up to and envelops the historical events of the New Testament, the church, and the modern world. History is grounded in the events recorded in Scripture. Moreover, history will some day culminate in the return of Christ to establish his kingdom here on earth and bring an end to the history begun with creation.

It is, of course, true that not all events in human history are recorded in the Bible—far from it! The Bible, however, is written in such a way as to include all possible history. Passages such as Daniel 2 and 7, for example, expand the events of Israel's history recorded in the Bible to include the course of historical events of all the succeeding nations and empires—right down to the time of the end of history. In the table of nations (Gen. 10), on the other hand, the histories of the nations of the world are linked, albeit succinctly, to the history of the descendants of Abraham. God's dealings with those nations are grounded in his election of Israel. History, therefore, is the record of God's great acts—centering in Creation and Redemption.

But history is also the record of humanity's not so great acts—the sad record of our great failures, beginning in the Garden of Eden (Gen. 2–3) and ending in the great revolt against God and his Messiah (cf. Ezek. 38–39; Rev. 17–19). But the Bible also tells of a history that will ultimately lead humanity back to God. Thus, history has a purpose—to lead humanity, the prodigal son, back to his gracious Father. Thus there is meaning to history's ceaseless tumults of suffering and pain, but a meaning recognizable only in Scripture.

A stunning picture of the end of human history is portrayed in Nebuchadnezzar's apocalyptic vision in Daniel 2. The great colossus of human history, with its gold head, silver shoulders, and bronze thighs gleaming in the sunlight, stood on iron feet mixed with clay. The world is crumbling beneath the weight of its own glory. All it takes for its demise is to be struck by a small rock that has dislodged itself from the towering hillside (2:36–45). That small rock is the coming kingdom of Christ. In the histories recorded in the Gospels, we see both the contrasts and the continuities between human history and God's ultimate purposes. Just as there was no place in Bethlehem for Jesus to be born (Luke 2:7), so there was no place for his kingdom among the kingdoms of this world. He died as the rejected "KING OF THE JEWS" (23:38). That death, however, marked the beginning of the end.

Miracles

The history recorded in the Bible is the story of real events. But those events are not simply about the ordinary affairs of humanity. They are about God's work in the lives of real men and women. Sometimes God works through natural means. In Genesis 18, for example, he sent three men to Abraham to announce the birth of his son Isaac. Abraham recognized God's presence in that simple human event (Gen. 18:3; see NIV note). This may be what the writer of Hebrews had in mind when he warned that "some people have entertained angels without knowing it" (Heb. 13:2).

But God is also at work in supernatural events, as when God sent fire and brimstone to destroy the cities of Sodom and Gomorrah (Gen. 19:24). The world depicted in the Bible is a world in which such miracles were at home. They were not common occurrences, to be sure, but when they happened they had a ready explanation—God was at work in his world.

What is a miracle? A miracle, in the biblical sense, is an event in nature that has its immediate cause from God himself, rather than the common laws of nature. A miracle occurs in nature; that is, it involves the natural world. When Moses struck the waters of the Red Sea and the waters dried up (Ex. 14:21–22), the people walked across the sea on dry ground. That was a miracle, but it happened within the natural world. God did not lead the people through a secret dimension of time and space so that they only appeared to walk on the dry ground. Rather, the sea actually parted, and the ground was dry.

Exodus 14 records "a strong east wind" that God caused to blow against the sea, divide its waters, and dry the ground. To say this is a miracle is to say that there were no meteorological preconditions to the strong east wind. Some claim that the real miracle in such biblical events lies in God's providential ordering of nature so that there were appropriate weather conditions at the time that caused the strong wind. Ultimately, such a line of thought reduces the idea of a miracle merely to a well-timed natural event. Though the biblical God is certainly capable of such timing, that is not the idea of miracles. A miracle involves the suspension of or free use of a natural law—as, for example, when an iron axhead floats in water (2 Kings 6:6) or when Jesus himself walked on water (Matt. 14:25).

Humanity and Redemption

The Image of God

The Bible states clearly that human beings are special creatures to God. When he created all the animals (Gen. 1:22), he created them "according to their kinds" (1:21). But when he created human beings, he made them "in his own image" (1:27). There is therefore a fundamental difference between these two forms of created life. The animals are important, indeed, precious to God. Jesus said, "Look at the birds of the air . . . your heavenly Father feeds them"; but, he continues, "Are you not much more valuable than they?" (Matt. 6:26). Human beings are the pinnacle of God's creation; among all the other creatures, they alone are like God.

What does it means to say that human beings were created in God's image? The Bible explains the image of God in two ways. (1) It is that aspect of our nature that makes us capable of knowing God personally. We are persons because God is a person. (2) It is that aspect of our nature that makes us capable of worshiping God. The worship of God by means of a man-made image is strictly forbidden because we as humans have been created in God's image. We were created to worship in his presence, not in the presence of a dumb idol.

The image of God gives human life its value and worth. Murder, for example, is expressly forbidden on the basis of our having been created in God's image (Gen. 9:6); so is cursing another human being (James 3:9). Human life is so valuable to God that he sent his own Son to give his life as a ransom for it (John 3:16).

What were human beings like before sin corrupted and tarnished God's image in the Fall? Human beings were "upright" (Eccl. 7:29) and "good" (Gen. 1:31). Their condition was analogous to the "new self" in Christ (Col. 3:10), who puts away "sexual immorality, impurity, lust, evil desires and greed" (3:5) and is clothed "with compassion, kindness, humility, gentleness and patience" (3:12). Being just and righteous before God, they were able to obey God's commands. It was possible for them not to sin. That is something that cannot be said of human beings today. For us today, after the Fall, it is impossible not to sin.

Impressed on the mind of the original man and woman, as a result of their being created in the image of God, was the law of God. That law mandated basic principles of justice, such as the distinction between right and wrong and the duty to worship God. A remnant of God's law still exists in our hearts today, showing "the requirements of the law are written on [our] hearts" (Rom. 2:14). The Bible calls this "conscience," which either accuses us of wrong or defends us when we are in the right (2:15).

The Fall

The Bible clearly teaches that the human race has fallen from its original state (Gen. 3). But the author of this account simply tells the story; he does not reflect on what transpired. We, the readers, are left to ourselves and our sense of the story to answer the questions it raises. We must seek our clues to its meaning from the story itself.

What then does this story teach us about the Fall? (1) The act that precipitated it was a transgression of God's will. God had simply said, "Do not eat of the tree," but the man and woman disobeyed. The consequences of that act were horrendous. (2) The man and the woman were cast out of the presence of God and were barred from access to the Tree of Life. This meant they began to experience both spiritual and physical death. (3) They became aware, in their nakedness, of the shame and guilt of their sin. Their attempt to cover their nakedness is a picture of all subsequent human attempts to cover over sin and its effects. (4) In their one act of disobedience, "sin entered the world . . . and death through sin" (Rom. 5:12), and "the result of one trespass was condemnation for all men" (5:18). (5) God was not the author of sin. He permitted the Fall, but the man and the woman, of their own volition, transgressed God's command. The serpent also played an important role. As an instrument of Satan (cf. Rev. 12:9), he, not God, was the one who tempted the first couple to sin.

How could the man and woman, created just and good, succumb to the temptation of the serpent and sin? It was not because they had been created with an evil inclination. It is rather that they were caught in the trap of wanting more than they had. They became greedy, wanting to be like God. Wanting to control their own destiny by obtaining the knowledge of good and evil, they were no longer willing to trust God. They had been created with the ability not to sin, but in the Fall it became impossible for them to do otherwise. They were now depraved. Furthermore, they passed that depravity on to all subsequent generations (Gen. 6:5). This is what is called "original sin." Note what David wrote: "Surely I was sinful at birth, sinful from the time my mother conceived me" (Ps. 51:5). Original sin is that corrupt disposition of the heart by which we are unable to do good and are prone to do evil. We are lost in our trespasses and are dead in our sins; only through Christ can those sins be forgiven (Col. 2:13).

What Is Sin?

Before answering this question from the viewpoint of the Bible, we do well to set it in the context of what various world religions and philosophies have said about the nature of sin. One common view (not represented by the Bible) is that sin is an essential part of the world, the necessary opposite of all that is good. This view of sin is so prevalent in human thinking that it has become an integral part of many religions, especially polytheistic religions (polytheism is the belief in many gods). These religions usually acknowledge good gods and evil gods, and they leave little room for ethical concepts such as ultimate goodness and righteousness.

The Bible, in presenting the view of ethical monotheism (the belief in the existence of only one God, who is the source of all that is good), does not recognize sin as an essential part of the world. Rather, sin is an intrusion into God's good creation. He did not create it as part of the world, nor did he cause it to enter the world. He did, however, permit sin to enter the world because, in his infinite wisdom, it was the only way to bring about his ultimate good, namely, his glory (Rom. 8:28).

Another view of sin found in human thinking, but not represented in the Bible, is that sin is somehow wrapped up in what it means to be human. God is infinitely good, but human beings simply are not. This view of sin is popular in modern theology. Sin, in effect, is reduced to simply being human—"to err is human." Such a view of sin, however, overlooks the fact that human beings were not created sinful. When they were created, God pronounced them "good" (Gen. 1:31), and sin as a human condition came only after an act of sin occurred (ch. 3).

Another popular view of sin is that it is anything that is enjoyable or gives pleasure. Such a view of sin is unfortunately often held by Christians. Somehow we think that if we are enjoying something too much, it must be wrong. Another wrong notion of sin views it as selfishness. That is, anything people do for themselves is a sin; they should always, and only, do things for others. Though selfishness is a sin, there are many things we do for ourselves that are not sinful.

Over against the false views of sin, the biblical idea is simple. Sin is an act of disobedience to the revealed will of God. When the first human beings chose to disobey God, they sinned. That one act of sin is played over again countless times in each of our daily lives.

The Effects of Sin

We present several points regarding the effects of sin on the human race today. (1) Sin is *universal*. It has affected every human being since the Fall. Adam and Eve's sin was transmitted, physically and legally, to all of their offspring. Along with that, the cultures and societies created by their offspring were necessarily products of the effects of sin. Thus, the environment within which humanity thrives and flourishes (that is, human culture) becomes a primary source of the contamination of sin. We have created contaminated environments, which, in turn, predispose us to sin. Human beings are like those who try to clean their houses but whose hands and equipment are dirty. The more they try to clean their surroundings, the worse off they seem to be.

(2) Sin is *total*. Human nature is "totally depraved." This means that there is not a single area or feature of our lives that has not been contaminated by sin. There is no "virgin soil" preserved from before the Fall within which to plant the seeds of a good life. Human nature has been warped or skewed away from conformity to God's will. But this does not mean humanity has lost all semblance of good. That is, "total" does not mean "complete." Much remains in human nature that is good. All human beings are capable of understanding beauty, compassion, love, and other aspects of our God-given nature. Like land around a contaminated nuclear power plant, our lives are capable of producing good fruit, but that fruit suffers from the same contamination of the land from which it arose.

(3) How does Adam's sin in the Garden of Eden reach our individual lives? We know, of course, that Adam's sin does affect our natures because we commit acts of sin. Moreover, the Bible clearly states that we are born in sin. David, for example, said, "Surely I was sinful at birth, sinful from the time my mother conceived me" (Ps. 51:5). But can we say, from Scripture, how this happens? The Bible presents two lines along which we may seek to understand the process. (a) There is in the Bible a kind of physical solidarity within the entire human race (Heb. 7:9–10). Just as an original in a copy machine imprints its imperfections on each copy, so Adam's sin is imprinted on us at birth. (b) More importantly, Adam is cast in the Bible as our representative. Just as an entire nation is implicated in decisions that its leaders make (e.g., to go to war), so in God's eyes, we are legally implicated in the sin of Adam (Rom. 5:12).

The Law

Talk of sin as disobedience to the will of God leads naturally to questions about the Law. The Law is the expressed will of God revealed to human beings. As early as the Garden of Eden, God told Adam and Eve that they could eat of all the trees of the Garden except "the tree of the knowledge of good and evil" (Gen. 2:16–17). As with most expressions of God's will, this first example is both positive and negative. God told them what they could do (eat from all the fruit trees) and what they could not do (eat from the tree of knowledge). But humanity was unwilling to obey God's law (Gen. 3). Nor is this an isolated story. The rest of the Bible is a testimony that "no one will be declared righteous in [God's] sight by observing the law" (Rom. 3:20).

Though it did not lead to their justification, God gave his people Israel an extensive written version of the Law at Mount Sinai (Ex. 19–Lev. 16). These laws were not the means for their salvation and blessing, in the sense that they could earn merits with God by obeying them. Their purpose was, rather, to keep them separate from the unbelieving world around them, to keep their worship of God pure from false practices, and to point to a time when God would send a Savior to redeem them, along with the rest of humanity, from the curse of sin (Gal. 3:15–24).

The Law, as a part of the Mosaic covenant, was thus a temporary measure. It pointed to the coming of a "new covenant" by which the Law, as God's expressed will, would be written on the heart of each man, women, and child of the covenant (Jer. 31:31–32). In the new covenant, God would not only write his Law on the human heart, but he would also pour out his Spirit on each member of the covenant and give them a "new heart" (Ezek. 36:26), by which they would "be careful to keep [his] laws" (36:27). According to the prophets, the new covenant would be established at the time of the coming of the Messiah and as part of his messianic kingdom.

The New Testament is clear that the coming of Jesus, and particularly his sacrificial death on the cross, established the new covenant (Luke 22:20). In his death, Jesus became our high priest, the mediator of the new covenant, as well as the sacrificial lamb whose blood was shed as the eternal offering for that covenant (Heb. 7:11–28). In Jesus and the new covenant we thus see the wish of Moses, the lawgiver, fulfilled (see Num. 11:29).

What does it mean for Christians to fulfill the Law? Does it mean keeping the dietary laws of Leviticus? Does it mean that those who break the Sabbath should be stoned (Num. 16:32–36)? Christians are not required to keep the Mosaic law as a means of grace (Rom. 6:14), but they are expected to live according to the basic moral law expressed there (8:4).

God's Plan of Redemption: The Old Testament

When God judged Adam and Eve immediately after the Fall, he also gave a word of promise and hope. God would not abandon them to find their own way back to him. He would send a Redeemer to crush the head of the serpent (Gen. 3:15) and thus restore humanity to the relationship with God they enjoyed before the Fall. As the Bible unfolds what the promise entailed, we gain an increasing understanding of God's great plan of redemption, which finds its fulfillment in Jesus Christ.

The promised Redeemer would be the "offspring" of the woman (Gen. 3:15), the offspring of Abraham (12:1–3), the offspring of Judah (49:8–12), and the offspring of David (2 Sam. 7:12–16). He was to come from the nation of Israel, God's chosen people (Neh. 9:7). He would be a king (Num. 24:7, 17) and would rule not only his own people, Israel, but also all the nations (Ps. 2:8). Through him all the nations would be blessed (72:17). He would receive his kingdom from God alone (Dan. 7:13–14; cf. 1 Chron. 17:14) and would establish that kingdom by defeating God's enemies in one last great battle (Dan. 7:26; Ezek. 38:7–23); after that God would restore the heavens and earth to their original state by creating them anew (Isa. 65:27). This King, though born a child, would be the "Mighty God" of Israel and would "reign on David's throne" forever (9:6–7).

But wait! There was one more detail in the original promise. The promised offspring of the woman would be fatally wounded. The serpent would "strike his heel" as he crushed the serpent's head (Gen. 3:15b). Someone had to die for the penalty of human rebellion (2:17). God promised to provide the sacrifice (22:8, 13–14). At first, the sacrifice was that of goats and bulls (Lev. 16:13–25), but they were insufficient for the sins of the people (Ps. 51:16). The promised King would offer himself as a sacrificial lamb (Isa. 53:7). He would be God's Servant, "pierced for our transgressions . . . crushed for our iniquities" (53:5).

What would happen after the death of this Servant-King? How could he die and yet reign forever on the throne of David? The afflicted Job foresaw the end of the promise: "I know that my Redeemer lives, and that in the end he will stand upon the earth" (Job 19:25). In other words, Job saw the resurrection of the Promised One. Similarly, David knew that God would not let his "Holy One see decay" (Ps. 16:10). Thus the coming King would "be raised and lifted up and highly exalted" (Isa. 52:13b) after "he bore the sin of many" (53:12).

God's Plan of Redemption: The New Testament

According to the New Testament, the Old Testament messianic promise is fulfilled in the life, death, resurrection, and glorious return of the Lord Jesus Christ. New Testament writers insist that Jesus is the promised King, born in a manger; the promised Prophet, rejected by his own people; and the promised Priest, who offered his own body as a sacrifice for humanity's sin. Jesus was born into the family of David, legally through Joseph (Matt. 1:6–16) and physically through Mary, herself a descendant of David (Luke 3:23–31). He was an heir to David's throne and an offspring of Judah, Abraham, and the woman. Jesus, the Redeemer, was a man.

But he was also the Son of God. At his birth, the angel Gabriel announced to Mary that "the Holy Spirit will come upon you, and the power of the Most High will overshadow you. So the holy one to be born will be called the Son of God" (Luke 1:35). He was given "the throne of his father David" and will reign forever (1:32–33). But Israel, the people of God, rejected their King (John 1:11). Hence, the kingdom was "taken away" from them and "given to a people who [would] produce its fruit" (Matt. 21:43).

Jesus informed his disciples that he as the Son of Man would suffer, be killed, after three days would rise again (Mark 8:31). On the evening of the Passover (John 18:28), when the lamb was to be slain (Matt. 27:46), Jesus was crucified, though like the Passover lamb, "not one of his bones [were] broken" (John 19:31–36; cf. Ex. 12:46). He was then buried. After three days, he rose from the dead (Luke 24:6) and ascended into heaven (Acts 1:9). Jesus then sent the Holy Spirit (2:33) to continue his work among his faithful Jewish followers (2:14–21) and the growing body of Gentiles (10:45). Through the missionary work of the apostles, the church spread through the ancient world, extending as far as Rome (28:30).

Jesus will some day return from heaven to establish his kingdom (Acts 1:11) "with power and great glory" (Matt. 24:30). The church still waits, with much anticipation, for that return (1 Cor. 15:50–58). He will come as a mighty warrior, defeating the forces of evil and finally crushing the head (Rev. 19:15) of "that ancient serpent called the devil, or Satan" (12:9; 20:2). When he comes, a great tribulation will break out on the earth (chs. 6–18), and all who are faithful to Jesus Christ will suffer in that persecution. At the end of seven years, those who have died in the persecution will be raised again to new life, and the kingdom established by Jesus will unite with God's people, Israel. Christ will rule over them as Messiah for a thousand years. After that there will be a second resurrection and a final judgment. Christ will then deliver the kingdom to the Father, and he will reign forever (1 Cor. 15:28).

Missions and Evangelism

When one surveys God's great plan of redemption, as we did in the previous sections, the question arises: What role does the individual Christian play in God's plan? Are we to sit back and watch it work, or is there a place for us in it? Historically, the recognition of God's plan and his work in the world has led to great enthusiasm and interest in world missions and evangelism. God intends to accomplish his work through individual members of the church. Christ's last words to his budding new church in Matthew was, "Go and make disciples of all nations. . . . And surely I am with you always, to the very end of the age" (Matt. 28:19–20). The book of Acts shows that it was the hope of the establishment of God's kingdom that drove Paul to constant missionary activity and zeal (Acts 28:31).

The concept of "missions," as well as the "mission" of the church, is central in the Bible. God created the human race, and his concern has been with humanity in its entirely, not just a segment of it. Even when God called Abraham to separate himself from the world and sojourn in Canaan (Gen. 12:1), it was for the purpose of bringing redemption and blessing to the rest of the world (12:2–3). God's actions for his people Israel always had the larger interest of the nations in mind. Even in hardening Pharaoh's heart so that he would not set the Israelites free, God did this so that "the Egyptians will know that [he is] the LORD" (Ex. 7:5). When God promised to establish a new covenant with Israel, its purpose was the salvation of the nations (Isa. 2:2–4).

Israel's "mission" was to be the means by which God blessed the nations. Abraham fulfilled that mission when he built altars and "called on the name of the LORD" wherever he set up his tent (e.g., Gen. 12:8). Abraham is thus the first "missionary," one who carried out the task of missions. That Israel did not successfully carry out their mission is made clear by the book of Jonah, a prophet who fled from his task to proclaim God's message to the great Gentile city of Nineveh. Of special importance is the reason Jonah gives for his reluctance. It was not because of fear, either of bodily harm or rejection; rather, it was because of Jonah's narrow particularism, for he wanted God's grace and blessing to extend only to his own country and his own people. The book of Jonah is written expressly to impugn such shortsightedness among God's people.

The Doctrine of Christ

The Person of Christ: His Incarnation

The Bible teaches the fact and the necessity of both Christ's human nature and his divine nature. For the promise of redemption to be fulfilled, the Redeemer of humanity had to be a human being, the offspring of a woman (Gen. 3:15). But for the death of the Redeemer to be effective, that is, of infinite value, he had to be God (see Heb. 9:11–12; 1 John 5:20). Underlying this necessity is the biblical concept of sacrifice: Life must be exchanged for life. The wages of sin is death (Gen. 2:17; Rom. 6:23), but "through the sacrifice of the body of Jesus Christ once for all" (Heb. 10:10) Jesus has become "the atoning sacrifice for our sins" (1 John 2:2).

Thus Jesus Christ is described as having both a human nature and a divine nature. The eternal Son of God, the second person of the Trinity, took upon himself a physical body and a human nature. This is the concept of the Incarnation ("becoming flesh"; cf. John 1:14). Nowhere, however, does the Bible explain how the two natures of Christ are linked, either to themselves or to the person of Christ. The explanation is derived by inference from statements in the Bible about Christ. The central concept in the Incarnation is called the "personal union" of Christ. The union of Christ's two natures is accomplished in the person of Christ himself—not in his natures.

In other words, we should not think of Christ as having two distinct persons with two distinct natures, as if two beings were united in a physical body. There is only one person—the eternal Son of God. When he clothed himself with a human body, he fully retained his divine nature. Both natures are united within the one eternal, divine person. Moreover, we should not think of this "personal union" as a mingling of two natures. Though united in the single person, the human and divine natures do not mix with one another. They are inseparably united, but distinct natures. Christ is fully God and fully human.

There is obviously a mystery here—just as there is a mystery in the way in which our own personalities are linked to our human nature. Philosophers and scientists have never been able to explain how the union of our own person and human nature happens within us, but we know it does. It is therefore not surprising that we cannot explain adequately how the two natures of Christ are united in him, but we know they have.

Two final points should be made about the person of Christ. (1) When he became a human being, he did not merely assume the body of someone who already existed. The Bible is clear that he was born into this world as the Son of God. (2) Christ's human nature, no less than his divine nature, was without sin.

The Person of Christ: His Exaltation

Where is Christ today, and what is he doing? The simple answer is that he is in heaven, awaiting his return to earth to establish his kingdom. The broader answer includes several key points. (1) Christ is now in heaven, still incarnate in his resurrected body. When Jesus rose from the dead, he became the first among all the dead to put on a new, restored human nature—one that not only consisted of the human nature God created in the beginning, but also one that is incorruptible and spiritual (1 Cor. 15:20; Col. 1:18).

(2) Thus, in his resurrection, Christ's humanity was raised to a new level from that of Adam's original state. Christ was the first among many to take on such a resurrected body. The believer's resurrected body will be a "spiritual body" (1 Cor. 15:44). Adam's body was made "from the dust of the ground" (Gen. 2:7; 1 Cor. 15:47), but our resurrection bodies will be "from heaven" (1 Cor. 15:47–49). Christ's body was a physical body, like Adam's, made for this earth; but unlike Adam's, it was also "spiritual," made for the new heavens and new earth promised in the last days (Rev. 21:1). His resurrection was not merely a return to life; it was a return to a new life and a new body. Note also that Christ's new body was the same as that which he had while here on earth, though it had now taken on immortality.

(3) When Christ returns, he will have the same resurrected body, as the angels testified to the apostles after Christ's ascension (Acts 1:11). At that time he will establish his kingdom (Rev. 22:3–5) and "reign on David's throne and over his kingdom, establishing and upholding it with justice and righteousness from that time on and forever" (Isa. 9:7). An important implication of this exaltation of Christ is that it shows that God views his creation as not only good in its original state (Gen. 1:31), but also, in its renewed state, as a worthy place for his dwelling forever with humanity (Rev. 21:3).

(4) In his exaltation to "the right hand of God" (Acts 2:33–36), Christ took on the role of the high priest interceding on behalf of the members of his church (Heb. 7:25), appearing "for us in God's presence" (9:24). That role is analogous to that of the high priest in the Mosaic covenant. The difference between Christ's work as a mediator and that of the high priests under the Mosaic covenant can be summarized in two words: Christ's role as high priest is *perfect* and *eternal*. It is perfect because Christ was, and is, sinless; it is eternal because Christ is the eternal second person of the Godhead (9:14). His perfect sacrifice consists of his own blood shed, once and for all, for us on the cross (9:12).

The Work of Christ: High Priest

In the context of the Old Testament, the Bible presents the work of Jesus Christ as that of a prophet, priest, and king. The next few sections discuss his work as priest. Jesus accomplished what the priesthood in ancient Israel could not do (Heb. 8:6); he offered his own body and blood as an eternal sacrifice for sin (10:10); and he intercedes with God on our behalf (Rom. 8:33).

Central to the biblical concept of Christ's work as priest is his role as high priest and mediator of our salvation. The need for a mediator, a "go-between," to speak and act both on God's part and on the part of human beings was established in the Old Testament. Moses was such a mediator. At Mount Sinai, when God appeared before the people in a blazing fire (Ex. 19:16), the people fled in fear and said to Moses: "Speak to us yourself and we will listen. But do not have God speak to us or we will die" (20:19). Only Moses stood before God (20:18–21). In that one act of courage or faith, the concept of the high priesthood was born.

As God's plans for Israel unfold in the Scriptures, the high priest, as mediator, became the means whereby atonement and sacrifice were made for the sins of the nation. This was represented most dramatically on the Day of Atonement (Lev. 16). Once each year, the high priest entered the tabernacle and the Most Holy Place and stood before the ark of the Lord. The tabernacle was a replica of heaven (Ex. 25:9); the ark, with its cover and guarding angels, represented the presence of the living God. God's holiness required special provisions to be made for covering the sins of the high priest as he entered God's presence. Those provisions included special sacred garments and special actions (e.g., ceremonial bathing). Most important, the high priest had to offer an animal sacrifice for his own sin. Otherwise he could not stand before a holy God: "Aaron [the high priest] shall bring the bull for his own sin offering to make atonement for himself and his household, and he is to slaughter the bull for his own sin offering" (Lev. 16:11).

Once he had entered the Most Holy Place and was standing before the ark, the high priest offered another animal sacrifice as "the sin offering for the people" (Lev. 16:15). In this way Israel could continue to experience God's holy presence in their midst in spite of their "uncleanness and rebellion" (16:16). By means of a number of further offerings, the high priest made atonement for the sins of the people. It was in assuming the role of high priest that Jesus offered himself as a sacrifice for the sins of the world (Heb. 9:11). To appreciate that role more fully, we must understand the concept of sacrifice.

Sacrifice

In the ceremonial laws God gave to ancient Israel, he provided a means of substitution whereby the death rightly due the sinful human being was transferred to an innocent animal. God accepted the blood shed by that animal and offered by the high priest as a substitute for the blood of the guilty sinner (cf. Lev. 17:11). Throughout the Old Testament, that system of sacrifice is assumed as God's gracious gift to atone for sin. It was already in use in the first stages of human society (Gen. 4). Noah offered sacrifices (8:20), as did the patriarchs: Abraham (12:7), Isaac (26:25), and Jacob (31:54). Thus, the sacrificial system established in the covenant at Mount Sinai was not new. In fact, as the Bible presents it, the notion of sacrificial substitution was established in God's plan before the creation of the world (1 Peter 1:19–20; Rev. 13:8).

An elaborate system of sacrifices and offerings is given in the book of Leviticus, where a sacrifice was the "substitution" of an animal for a sinful person or community. A full explanation of how and why sacrifices were effective in dealing with human sin is not spelled out in the Bible. It was simply assumed that God's holiness had to receive some compensation for the offense of human sin, that the means to accomplish this was sacrifice, and that God accepted such sacrifices.

Moreover, the Bible does not present sacrifice, in and of itself, as the effective means of removing sin and guilt. There were no magical powers in the sacrifice. It "worked" only because God accepted it. As in the case of the first record of sacrifices and offerings of Cain and Abel (Gen. 4), God accepted the offering because he knew the heart of the one who offered it.

Throughout the Old Testament, a noticeable inequity was felt in its system of sacrifices. David, for example, wrote: "O Lord ... you do not delight in sacrifice, or I would bring it; you do not take pleasure in burnt offerings" (Ps. 51:15–16). As the New Testament reflected on the Old, it recognized that it was "impossible for the blood of bulls and goats to take away sins" (Heb. 10:4). For example, the constant repetition of the sacrifices of the old covenant to cover the guilt of the people implied that something more effective or more permanent was needed. That something was "the sacrifice of the body of Jesus Christ once for all" (10:10). A parallel theme is found in Isaiah 53:5–11, whereby a chosen Servant of God would bear the sins of the people in his own death. Jesus was the sacrificial Lamb of God (cf. 1 Peter 1:19), "the atoning sacrifice for our sins" (1 John 2:1).

Satisfaction

When Jesus Christ died on the cross, the full force of God's wrath against sin and rebellion was directed against him personally. His death satisfied God's righteous anger, in which God was once and for all eternity exhausted of his anger. He, as it were, had no more wrath from which to vent his hatred of sin. God was eternally satisfied when his Son suffered that infinitely horrible death.

The idea of divine satisfaction is a difficult concept for modern Christians to appreciate because we do not have a clear notion of God's wrath. Modern Christians are all too familiar with the positive side of the gospel—God's mercy and grace in forgiving sin. There is, however, another side. Human sin must receive its due recompense. It cannot be swept under a cosmic rug in God's universe. The very fact that God sent his own Son, Jesus, to die an excruciating death on the cross should alert us to the fact that God treats sin seriously. If it had been possible for him to look the other way and ignore human sin, he would surely have done so. But he did not.

To understand what it means that Christ's death "satisfied" God's wrath, we must note the Bible's own clear statements about God's hatred of sin. Paul says, "The wrath of God is being revealed from heaven against all the godlessness and wickedness of men" (Rom. 1:18). The wrath of God is his anger, but it is not simply that. His wrath and hatred of sin are grounded in his own holiness and righteousness. Sin has no place in God's good universe, which has now been contaminated by sin (Gen. 3; Rom. 3:23), and its presence could not be long tolerated by an eternal and infinitely just Creator. God's wrath is thus his righteous recoil from sin, and "satisfaction" is his once and for all eternal removal of the grounds for that wrath.

The Bible refers often to God's wrath and the need for satisfaction. The sin of idolatry, for example, was "satisfied" by a complete razing of the city in which it was found (see Deut. 13:12–17). God compares the razed city here to a "burnt offering," suggesting that behind the burning of a sacrifice was a display of his wrath that had thereby been satisfied. This passage also shows that "satisfaction" is not a matter of "buying off" God, appeasing his anger, or making God feel good again. Rather, satisfaction is simply God's only possible response to sin. He had to give it its just reward—eternal punishment. That is why Christ died on the cross.

The Sacrificial System and Christ

According to the New Testament, the various parts of the tabernacle, the priesthood, and the sacrifices in the Pentateuch were "a copy and shadow" of God's heavenly abode (Heb. 8:5). This idea comes from the Old Testament itself. In the instructions for building the tabernacle, for example, Moses is told to follow closely the "pattern" he received from God on Mount Sinai (Ex. 25:40). Curiously, the builder of the tabernacle was Bezalel, whose name in Hebrew means "In the shadow of God." But the Old Testament itself explains little of the heavenly meaning of the tabernacle and its parts, how they exhibit the pattern of the heavenly temple and point to Christ. There is thus a mysterious element to the tabernacle.

But we do have the finished work of Christ to guide us, though we must proceed carefully. The Law itself was "only a shadow of the good things that are coming—not the realities themselves" (Heb. 10:1). Furthermore, the New Testament understands the religious feasts and festivals in the Old Testament as "a shadow of the things that were to come; the reality, however, is found in Christ" (Col. 2:17). In other words, God's purpose in giving Israel the ceremonial law was to "prefigure" the coming of Christ.

A "figure" is a person, place, or action in the Old Testament that foreshadows something about Christ in the New Testament. The apostle Paul, for example, speaks of the crossing of the Red Sea as a figure of Christian baptism (1 Cor. 10:1–2). The gathering and eating of the manna in the desert is a picture of the nourishment the Holy Spirit gives to the church (10:3–4). Lest we think that such an understanding of the Old Testament is simply a way to read Christian ideas back into these texts, we should pay close attention to passages like Nehemiah 9:20, where the giving of manna is also identified with God's sending his Spirit. Thus the Old Testament itself draws spiritual lessons from the persons and events recorded therein.

According to a common line of Christian interpretation, the ark (Ex. 25:10–22) is often understood as a figure of Christ. That it was made of wood prefigures Christ's partaking of the physical world in his Incarnation. The gold overlay that covered the wood of the ark prefigures his divine nature. The symbolic value of placing the testimony (Scripture) inside the ark is usually taken to show that Christ is the mediator of the covenant and has the law written within his heart (cf. Ps. 40:8; Jer. 31:33). Finally, the New Testament itself takes the "atonement cover" (Ex. 25:17) as a picture of Christ's "sacrifice of atonement" (Rom. 3:25).

The Work of Christ: King

As a king, Jesus gathers and establishes his reign among God's people—today the church, and in the future the whole world; he cares for and blesses his people with eternal life (John 10:28); and he protects his reign against the enemies of darkness (Rom. 16:20).

The Old Testament concept of "messiah" is synonymous with the notion of kingship. The patriarch Jacob proclaimed that the right of the kingship would "not depart from Judah, nor the ruler's staff from between his feet, until he comes to whom it belongs" (Gen. 49:10). Balaam foresaw the rise of a King of Israel who would defeat Israel's enemies and establish a worldwide kingdom (Num. 24:17–24). Hannah prayed that God would send that King to defeat the enemy and judge the world in her own day (1 Sam. 2:10). When David became the first king of Judah, many hoped he would be the promised King. Those hopes were quickly put to rest by Nathan, who prophesied that one of David's descendants would establish his house and throne forever (2 Sam. 7:12–16).

Throughout the years of the monarchy in Israel and Judah, hope began to wane that God's word would be fulfilled through the house of David. Only a few kings were God-fearing, and when Jerusalem was destroyed and the people exiled to Babylon, all hope in the fulfillment of the promise to David was lost. But the prophets still claimed that God would not only reestablish the people of Israel in the Promised Land; he would also send a King to the house of David to rule over Israel and the nations.

The fullest expression of that new vision is Daniel 7:11–14. The messianic Son of Man is seen coming in the clouds of heaven to receive an eternal kingdom from God. This Son of Man "was given authority, glory and sovereign power; all peoples, nations and men of every language worshiped him. His dominion is an everlasting dominion." For Daniel, the fulfillment of God's promise to David was to be found in an eternal heavenly kingdom that God would bring to earth.

At the birth of Jesus, many in Israel were eagerly awaiting the fulfillment of these promises. An angel came to a young woman of the house of David to announce the birth of the King (Luke 1:26). When Jesus was born, the faithful of Israel recognized him as the promised King (2:25–32). Jesus himself proclaimed that the kingdom of God was at hand (Matt. 12:28), and he was welcomed into Jerusalem as the reigning King (21:1–9). But he was rejected by Israel (21:42–46), and the kingdom taken away (21:43). Nevertheless, at the "end of the age" (24:3), the Son of Man will come again as King "with power and great glory" (Matt. 24:30).

The Work of Christ: Prophet

Christ's work entailed the prophetic office. A prophet is a messenger who speaks for God. He represents God to his people and to the nations. Already in the book of Deuteronomy, God promised to raise up a "prophet like [Moses]" (Deut. 18:15, 18), though this promise was general enough to apply to the entire prophetic office during the days of the Israelite theocracy. God raised up many prophets who spoke for him and who chided the people when they went astray. As those prophets came and went, however, the expectation grew that a specific "prophet like Moses" would arise, who would also fill the office of the messianic king and priest promised in the Scriptures. His coming would be announced by the return of the prophet Elijah, who would lead God's people in obeying the law of Moses and thus prepare them for the establishment of God's kingdom (Mal. 4:4–6). When the office of prophet ceased to function in Israel, a later biblical writer added a note to the end of Deuteronomy, showing that many in Israel were still awaiting the arrival of the coming prophet: "Since then, no prophet has risen in Israel like Moses" (Deut. 34:10). The hope of the coming prophet was still alive.

The New Testament writers take great pains to show that Jesus was the prophet promised to Moses. Jesus was, in fact, a new Moses. The Gospel of Matthew presents him as God's spokesman, who, like Moses, gave God's word to his people on a mountain (Matt. 5–7). Like Moses, menacing events preceded Jesus' birth (Ex. 1:22; Matt. 2:16), and he had to remain in Egypt, awaiting the time of his entry into the land (Ex. 2; Matt. 2:13). Moses spent forty years in the desert, and Jesus spent forty days. Moses crossed the Red Sea as his baptism in preparation for his ministry (1 Cor. 10:1–2); Jesus crossed through the Jordan River as his baptism in preparation for this ministry (Matt. 3:13–17). During Moses' ministry, the birth of Jesus was predicted by a wise man from the east, the seer Balaam, who saw the coming of Christ as a "star [coming] out of Jacob" (Num. 24:17). At the birth of Jesus, wise men came from the east, "who saw his star in the east and [came] to worship him" (Matt. 2:1–2).

In John's Gospel, the woman at the well recognized Jesus as a prophet (John 4:19) and concluded he was the Messiah (4:25), a statement that Jesus confirmed (4:26; cf. also 6:14; 7:40). It is little wonder, then, that in the book of Revelation, John also identifies Jesus as the promised prophet who reveals to his churches "what will take place later" (Rev. 1:19; cf. Matt. 24:25).

The Doctrine of the Holy Spirit

The Holy Spirit Is a Person

God, by his very nature, is a spiritual being (John 4:24). The word "spirit" means "without bodily form or substance." But within the three persons of the Godhead, there is one person who is distinctly called "the Spirit of God" or "the Holy Spirit."

The Bible reveals both the existence and work of the Spirit. He was integrally involved in God's work in creation (Gen. 1:2). God's Spirit equipped Israel's artisans with the skill they needed to build the tabernacle (Ex. 31:3). He empowered Israel's leaders (Num. 27:18) and gave them wisdom to guide God's people in the way they should go (11:17; Deut. 34:9). He also enabled God's prophets to prophesy (Num. 11:25) and speak forth God's word to the people (Neh. 9:30). The Holy Spirit empowered Christ in his earthly ministry (Luke 3:22; 4:1, 14, 18; 10:29; 11:13; 12:10; Acts 1:2; 10:38) and founded the church by indwelling each of its members (Acts 2:4; 1 Cor. 12:13). When, after his resurrection, Christ ascended to the right hand of the Father, he "poured forth" the Spirit on all those who called on his name (Acts 2:33).

The Spirit of God is not simply a divine impulse or force by which God interacts with the world. He is a real and distinct person. This is seen in a technical sense in how the New Testament refers to the Holy Spirit. In the Greek language, the word "spirit" is a neuter noun. Technically, then, the New Testament writers should refer to the Spirit as an "it." Instead, they consistently refer to the Spirit of God as "he," just as they would a person. Note John 15:26, for example: "When the Counselor comes, whom I will send to you from the Father, the Spirit of truth who goes out from the Father, *he* [not it] will testify about me." John treats the Spirit sent from the Father as a distinct person (cf. 16:13–14). In Acts 13:2 the Holy Spirit speaks as a person, saying "Set apart for me Barnabas and Saul for the work to which I have called them." This view of the Spirit is commensurate with the many passages in Scripture that speak of the Holy Spirit performing all kinds of personal actions and works (for example, John 16:13; Acts 15:28; 1 Cor. 2:10; 12:11).

One important implication of the personhood of the Holy Spirit is that by means of his work in the life of the Christian, he enables us to have *personal* fellowship with God (Rom. 8:26). Because the Holy Spirit is a person, he is able to intercede and commune with Christians on behalf of the Father and the Son (John 14:23–24).

The Work of the Holy Spirit (Old Testament)

The main work of the Spirit of God throughout Scripture is to accomplish God's will. A central feature of God's purpose in Scripture is the task of establishing his kingdom in the world. That work was accomplished "in the beginning," when God first set out to establish his kingdom (Gen. 1:2). When disobedience and sin resulted in the dissolution of God's rule in the world (3:6–19), again the Spirit's task was to bring about its restoration. Within Scripture, then, the work of the Spirit concentrated on God's covenant promises to Israel, through which God intended to reestablish his kingdom. Within that program, the Spirit was called upon to empower divinely selected individuals to carry out God's plan.

We first see the Spirit of God at work within the Sinai covenant where he miraculously bestowed on Israel's artisans the skill they needed to make the utensils and furnishings needed for the tabernacle (Ex. 31:1–3). The artisan Bezalel was filled with the Spirit for this task. When the task of administering God's covenant laws among the people obviously became too much for one person to handle, God selected seventy elders to help Moses administer the law and gave them his Spirit to enable them to carry out their work (Num. 11:16–17).

During the time of the judges, before the rise of the divinely appointed king, God sent his Spirit to empower Israel's leaders in times of trouble (cf. Judg. 3:10; 6:34; 11:29; 13:25; 14:6, 19; 15:14). When the Israelites requested a king to replace these judges, God selected Saul and empowered him with his Spirit (1 Sam. 10:9–10). And when Saul was rejected as king, God took his Spirit from Saul (16:14) and sent him on David (16:13). Henceforth, the mark of divine leadership among the people of God was the presence of the Spirit. When David himself sinned and cried out to God for forgiveness, one central plea was that God not take his Spirit from him (Ps. 51:11). David wanted the privilege of continuing as God's anointed leader.

Israel's kings became less and less fit instruments of God's power. Thus the Spirit of God raised up prophets to confront the kings and the people with their apostasy (Zech. 7:12). Even though the people rejected the words of the prophets, the latter fulfilled their task by means of God's Spirit. When God's people were sent into captivity, the prophets began to foretell how God would pour out his Spirit on all humanity and establish his universal kingdom (Ezek. 36:26–27; Joel 2:28–32). According to the New Testament, Jesus is the long-awaited Messiah, fulfilling the prophetic promise of the Spirit (Acts 2:16).

The Work of the Holy Spirit (New Testament)

The New Testament writers clearly portray that the coming of the Spirit at Pentecost and the establishment of the church as a direct consequence of God's promise in the Old Testament to send the Spirit on his people. Before his death and resurrection, Jesus told his disciples about the coming role of the Holy Spirit as a "Counselor" of God's people (John 16:7), who would teach believers and guide them in the truth (16:12–15) and who would "convict" the ungodly world of their sin and of God's impending judgment (16:8–11). When Jesus ascended to the Father, he gave the Holy Spirit to the fledgling new community of believers. At that time, the church consisted of a remnant of Jewish believers gathered in Jerusalem. They saw themselves as a fulfillment of the Old Testament promises (cf. Acts 2:16).

Not all went as expected, however. Though a sizable Jewish remnant did believe in Jesus as their Messiah and promised King, the nation as a whole rejected him (Acts 3:13–16). Thus, the establishment of Christ's kingdom would have to await the repentance and faith of God's people Israel (3:20–21).

But what must come of God's promise of the Spirit? What does Israel's rejection of the Messiah mean for the coming of the Holy Spirit at Pentecost? Paul argues in Romans 9–11 that Israel's rejection of Jesus as their Messiah was intended in God's plan to open the door of blessing and salvation to the Gentiles (Rom. 11:11–24). Luke argues the same point in Acts, for even though the nation of Israel rejected Jesus (Acts 4:11), the church continued to grow. Ultimately, the Spirit of God was "poured out even on the Gentiles" (10:44–45). Luke closes Acts by showing that the Jewish rejection of Jesus had been already foretold by the Holy Spirit through the prophets (28:25).

As the Spirit had done among the Israelites in the Sinai covenant, he began to do with the church. After Christ's ascension into heaven, he gave the gifts of the Spirit to the church (Eph. 4:7–13), including a whole array of supernatural gifts (1 Cor. 12:4–11). It is now no longer a few select individuals who are empowered by God's Spirit, as it had been under the old covenant, but each and every believer receives that Spirit (Rom. 8:9–10). Moses' wish that all God's people be given a portion of his Spirit (cf. Num. 11:29) has been fulfilled.

The new work of the Spirit within the church involves a permanent indwelling of each believer (John 14:16–17). His task is primarily to glorify Christ (14:16) and, in Christ's absence, to bear witness to him to the believer (15:26). Furthermore, the work of the Spirit is to empower believers to transform lives through the preaching of the gospel (14:12).

Salvation

The Meaning of Salvation

The biblical understanding of salvation consists of several interrelated factors. At its heart, however, is *justification*, which means that an individual sinner is accounted righteous before God, not on his or her own merits, but on the merits of Christ's own righteousness offered to the Father on our behalf. The work of justification, then, is a divine act applied to the individual Christian.

The other important factors in the biblical view of salvation include: (1) conversion—the transformation of the heart of a sinner from rebellion against God to obedience and faith; (2) faith—an act of trust and dependence on God and his Word; (3) regeneration—the spiritual birth of a dead sinner, by which God is able to accomplish a new work; (4) sanctification—the progressive transformation of the individual sinner into an obedient and faithful Christian; and (5) perseverance—the uninterrupted process of sanctification.

Christian theology lays great stress on each of these factors, seeking to understand them not only in their own right but also in terms of their relationship to one another. The segments that follow discuss each factor separately; here our attention focuses on the relationship of each to the others. We must first make an important distinction, for we can talk about their interrelationship in two ways. (1) Temporally: We can ask, "Which comes first?" (2) Logically: We can ask, "Which is more basic?" To ask the temporal question is like asking, "Which came first, the chicken or the egg?" Obviously, we cannot have a chicken without the egg, but we need a chicken to lay the egg. Thus, the temporal question cannot be resolved. But if we ask, "Which is more basic, the chicken or the egg?" it is apparent that it is the chicken. Regardless of where the chicken came from, it is more basic than the egg.

In addressing the question of the interrelationship of the various factors of salvation, it is more productive to try to understand the logical relationships than the temporal ones. For the most part our salvation is a single, simultaneous act of God. God does not reason as human beings do, resolving one issue and then moving to another. His thoughts are infinite and his reasoning instantaneous. Thus, the question of timing is irrelevant. The important question is that of the logical relationship between the factors of salvation. In theological jargon, the question of this interrelationship is called "the order of salvation" (*ordo salutis*).

The Order of Salvation (*Ordo Salutis*)

We have just discussed the general notion of salvation and the question of the "order" of its various factors. Now we take a closer look at how Christian theologians have attempted to resolve the order question. But if, as suggested above, God's act of salvation is simultaneous, why worry about the order at all? The answer is that, though the temporal order is not important, the logical relationship is. Our understanding of the process of salvation depends on the logical relationship that exists, in God's mind, between the factors of salvation.

There are two basic views on the logical sequence of salvation, the *ordo salutis*: the Reformed view (generally considered more precise and logically correct) and the Arminian view (more widely held). (1) The Reformed view begins with the idea that Adam's sin is inherited by every individual at birth, so that everyone is born dead in sin. That being the case, God must first, logically, give one a new life (regeneration) before any work at all can be accomplished in his or her heart. After God has called and regenerated the individual sinner, he or she can then turn away from sin and to God (conversion). This step entails repentance and faith. When the sinner repents and believes in Christ, God reckons him or her righteous (justification). The logical consequence of being accounted righteous is living a holy life, so that sanctification follows justification. If one's justification and sanctification are genuine, then the person will persevere in salvation.

(2) The Arminian view of the order of salvation differs from the Reformed view at the outset by removing the transmission of Adam's sin as an inherited factor. Rather, Adam's sin was dealt with and removed in the death of Christ, so that individuals are born into a fallen world with human natures contaminated by Adam's sin, but they are not dead. They are still able to act and thus choose to do good. God's grace is such that each person born into this world can, if he or she wills, choose to accept God's offer of salvation. The order of salvation thus begins, logically, with a divine act of universal grace whereby all of humanity can choose God's gift of salvation. Faith, as a free act of the individual sinner, is the consequence of God's gracious offer. On the basis of that faith, God accounts the sinner righteous and begins the work of rebirth and renewal of the sinner's heart (regeneration). This leads to the Christian's perseverance.

Regeneration

Simply put, *regeneration* is the process whereby spiritually dead sinners are made alive by God's Spirit. A dead soul is given new life. The premise on which the concept of regeneration operates is that humanity is born spiritually dead. All have died in Adam. For there to be spiritual life, therefore, there must be a spiritual rebirth.

Who is responsible for regeneration? It hardly needs saying that individual human beings are not responsible for their own regeneration. When Jesus told Nicodemus that he must be born again, Nicodemus replied, "How can one be born when he is old? . . . Surely he cannot enter a second time into his mother's womb to be born!" (John 3:4). He recognized it was impossible to be born again physically, let alone spiritually. But Jesus told him that what was impossible with man was possible with God. The Spirit can give one new life (3:6); regeneration is an act of God's Spirit.

What is the basis of regeneration? Once again, there are, at least logically, two views to this question. The Reformed view is that God's sovereign call (that is, election) is the basis of regeneration; God regenerates those whom he calls. Regeneration thus precedes faith and justification. The Arminian view, on the other hand, is that God regenerates those who turn to him in faith. Regeneration thus follows faith and justification.

Though the idea is found throughout Scripture, the word "regeneration" occurs only once, in Titus 3:5. There it seems clear that regeneration comes solely on the basis of God's mercy: "[God] saved us, not because of righteous things we had done, but because of his mercy. He saved us through the washing of rebirth [regeneration] and renewal by the Holy Spirit." Both the Reformed and Arminians find support in this passage. The former say that by God's mercy the individual was called and thus regenerated. The latter say that by his mercy God gave the individual sufficient grace to believe in the gospel and thus experience regeneration.

What is the result of regeneration? In the Reformed view, regeneration results in the ability to see and believe the gospel and thus turn to God in faith. A dead person cannot see and understand the gospel, let alone believe it. Regeneration produces the necessary spiritual life to do so. According to the Arminian view, regeneration leads to sanctification. It is the new spark of spiritual life that must grow into the regenerate believer.

What is the extent of regeneration? Both the Reformed and Arminian views understand regeneration to be only the beginning of the process of spiritual growth, not its final goal.

Faith

The biblical concept of *faith* is best seen by realizing that the primary word for faith in the Bible is the Hebrew verb "to believe." This word basically means "to trust." For example, this verb is linked to the notion of a small child who rests in the arms of its nursemaid, or it is related to steadfastness and strength. To believe in someone is to trust that person. It is to rest in his or her care as a young child in the arms of its mother. It is to remain steadfast and strong in one's commitment. That view of faith carries over into the New Testament. Faith is more than merely assenting to the truths of the gospel, though that is involved. Faith is also putting one's trust in Christ's provision for our salvation.

Who is responsible for faith? Is it something we must do on our own in order to receive salvation, or is it a gift from God? Passages such as Ephesians 2:8 ("For it is by grace you have been saved, through faith ... it is the gift of God") make it clear that faith is a gift from God.

What is the relationship between faith and works? The Bible often compares and contrasts the notion of faith with "works." Biblical writers state that faith and trust in God must not be confused with trying to earn God's favor by our own good deeds. God, of course, is deeply concerned that Christians live righteously. But when it comes to our personal salvation, good works may not replace a simple trust in God's provision. As Isaiah says (Isa. 64:6), "All our righteous acts are like filthy rages." We must rely on what God has done for us.

Has faith always been the means whereby one may accept God's provision of salvation? The Bible's answer is a clear yes. Genesis 15:6 reads, "Abraham believed the LORD, and he credited it to him as righteousness." Even under the Mosaic covenant, when Israel was commanded to obey every letter and detail of the law, faith was the basis of their acceptance with God. The Israelites were given signs to believe in when Moses brought them out of Egypt (Ex. 4:5). When they saw the signs Moses and Aaron performed, "they believed" (4:29–31). And when the people failed "to believe" God, as in their refusal to take the Promised Land when God told them to, an entire generation missed out on God's blessing and provision (Num. 14:11). The centrality of faith through God's dealings with Israel and the nations is clearly exhibited in Hebrews 11.

Justification

The central idea of *justification* is expressed in the passage that speaks of Abraham's faith being "credited ... to him as righteousness" (Gen. 15:6). The word "credited" means simply that God "considered" him righteous. Justification is an act of God whereby he "considers" the sinner as righteous. God does not look at the sinner and see righteousness inside him or her. Rather, he looks at the sinner and, though seeing a sinner, considers that person righteous.

To be righteous, in biblical terms, means being in conformity with God's standard of what is right. God is righteous when he conforms to his own standard. When Israel transgressed God's covenant, God brought judgment on them—the punishment rightly due them for their unrighteousness. Isaiah, for example, speaks of the destruction that God decreed on Israel as "overwhelming and righteous" (Isa. 10:22b). When Daniel surveys Israel's long history of disobedience and God's judgment, he concludes, "Lord, you are righteous, but this day we are covered with shame ... because of our unfaithfulness to you" (Dan. 9:7–8).

Legally, to pronounce someone "not guilty" of a charge—that is, to acquit someone—is to justify that person. The term by itself does not mean that the person acquitted is, in fact, "not guilty." It says only that the person was legally *considered* "not guilty." Note that it is possible to acquit (or justify) a guilty person. But if we as guilty persons are justified, something has to be done with our guilt. In God's process of justification, this guilt is placed on Christ, and Christ's righteousness is placed on us. Thus, *to justify* means simply to declare us righteous, whether or not we are, in reality, innocent of the charge. When God "justifies the wicked" (Rom. 4:5), he declares the ungodly to be righteous in his sight by crediting Christ's righteousness to them.

One can see that the biblical idea of justification is strictly a legal term. The inward condition of the justified person is not affected by an influx of righteousness (in this way, justification is different from regeneration, by which a person is inwardly changed and renewed). When God justifies a sinner, that sinner is a regenerate sinner—but a sinner in need of God's grace and of being justified.

In addition to being regenerated, a justified person has also begun the process of being sanctified; thus, he or she will begin to produce fruits that reflect the new status as justified. This is another way in which human beings can be called righteous, insofar as they do what is right. But that meaning of righteousness is a fruit of justification, not a requirement for salvation.

Perseverance

A frequently asked question about the Christian life is: "Can a person lose his or her salvation?" People rarely ask this question about themselves. Anyone concerned enough to ask such a question usually does so within the context of a sincere commitment of faith. People usually have in mind a loved one or friend who once professed faith in Christ but who now has cast it aside or who has drifted away from the Lord. They want assurance that their loved one or friend is saved. Embedded in this question are many assumptions about the nature of the other person's faith and outward life. But the question is often so misdirected that a straight answer is impossible.

It is impossible to judge the genuineness of another person's faith. Only God knows the heart (cf. 1 Sam. 16:7). The basic principle by which we may judge the true intentions of others is laid down by Christ, "By their fruit you will recognize them" (Matt. 7:16; cf. Gal. 5:16–24). How can we know for sure that another's faith is genuine or not? We cannot. We must take them at their word, and we must look at the fruit that their lives produce.

But we may not build our understanding of the nature of salvation on such uncertain examples. We must start with the assumption that the faith we are talking about is genuine faith. Can one lose that kind of faith? As might be expected, there is no single answer to that question. The Reformed answer is that one cannot lose genuine faith. Faith comes solely to the elect, and one cannot become "unelect." Genuine faith will persevere because that faith, from the start, is a work of God in the believer's heart. As Paul wrote, "He who began a good work in you will carry it on to completion until the day of Christ Jesus" (Phil. 1:6). Such faith will grow and produce good fruit. The absence of fruit is not a sign of a faith that was lost, but that faith was never there at all.

Arminians, however, answer the question differently. They see faith from the human side and point to other statements in Paul's letters that warn of not remaining firm in one's faith (see Col. 1:23). Such warnings, they say, are enough to question whether genuine faith will persevere if neglected or ignored. These warnings, however, do not explicitly state that one would ever do such a thing. For the most part, such passages are to be understood as exhortations to exercise our faith, not as threats about losing faith. In the last analysis, such biblical warnings should cause all true Christians to heed Paul's advice, "Examine yourselves to see whether you are in the faith" (2 Cor. 13:5).

Sanctification

Sanctification is the divine process by which Christians become more and more like Christ. It is a divine process because the changes in the life of the Christian are produced by the Holy Spirit (1 Peter 1:2). Those changes are not the result of self-improvement efforts or reimaging. They are the result of the power of God renewing the heart and mind of the Christian. Paul writes the power at work in the Christian's life "is like the working of his mighty strength, which [God] exerted in Christ when he raised him from the dead" (Eph. 1:19–20). In the Christian's sanctification, God's resurrection power is at work on a renewal project.

The goal of sanctification is the likeness of Christ because in him God has demonstrated his purpose in creating humanity in God's image (Gen. 1:26; Col. 1:15). The aim of the Christian's life is to "grow up into him who is the Head, that is, Christ" (Eph. 4:15). The model is the life of Christ; the means is the Holy Spirit; the method is a daily walk with God through prayer, Bible study, Christian fellowship, and worship. This sort of life is a "living sacrifice" and, when lived "holy and pleasing to God," a "spiritual act of worship" (Rom. 12:1).

God wants us to "be sanctified" (1 Thess. 4:3), which means putting away all forms of immorality and impurity and living a "holy life" (4:3–7). The word *sanctification*, in fact, means "made holy." A believer's sanctification begins the moment he or she is regenerated and continues until the end of his or her life. Regeneration is instantaneous, but sanctification is a process, one that is never complete in this life. Christians eagerly await the final redemption of the body, which comes either with death or the return of Christ (Rom. 8:22–23).

Sanctification is commonly viewed as a struggle between two forces at work in the life of the Christian: the old nature and the new nature. The new person is the regnerate, new person, born again in Christ. The Christian's new nature desires to do God's will, but the old nature refuses to go along. There is warfare within the Christian's heart (see Rom. 7:15–24; Gal. 5:17), but with God's help, the new nature eventually overcomes the old. In both Romans 7:25 and Galatians 5:22–25, Paul concludes on the note of victory over sin in this life through the power of the Holy Spirit; "the law of the Spirit of life has set me free from the law of sin and death" (Rom. 8:2). Does the Christian ever completely overcome his or her old nature? The Bible gives little hope of that, this side of heaven.

Good Works

The topic of the Christian's sanctification leads naturally to the question of good works. What role do they play in the life of the believer? The phrase *good works* is in some ways misleading. The central thrust of the gospel is that God has offered justification "by faith apart from works of the Law" (Rom. 3:28 NASB). The very mention of "works" thus seems out of place in a discussion of the gospel. For that reason, we want to make it clear that in this context, "good works" does not refer to "works of law" as a means of obtaining salvation. We are rather speaking of "good actions" that grow out of the Christian's new life in Christ. It is perhaps preferable to talk about "good acts of faith." They are the result of and a sign of the Christian's new life.

The first and most important question is whether good works are necessary for salvation. Most non-Christians seem to view Christianity as a works-oriented religion. They think that if you live a good enough life, God will let you into heaven when you die. Such a view, however, is a far cry from what we find in the Bible. No one is ever good enough to be admitted into heaven. "There is no one righteous, not even one. . . . There is no one who does good, not even one" (Rom. 3:10–12). If good works alone justified us before God, heaven would be a lonely place.

Where, then, does the notion that works are important for salvation come from? Simply put, it comes from the central role that good works play in the Christian life. The Bible states clearly that even though good works will not justify a sinner, those who are justified will produce good works. The Bible sounds the theme that "faith without deeds is dead" (James 2:25; cf. v. 17). The Israelite prophets continually warned the people that good works arising out of a pure heart were essential in their ongoing walk with the Lord. The prophet Micah put that message succinctly: "[God] has showed you, O man, what is good. And what does the LORD require of you? To act justly and to love mercy and to walk humbly with your God" (Mic. 6:8). Micah was speaking of the importance of living a life that reflects God's will. As Samuel once warned the disobedient Saul, "To obey [God] is better than sacrifice" (1 Sam. 15:22).

What role do good works play in our salvation? They are never meritorious—that is, they never deserve credit before God. Rather, (1) good works are evidence of our salvation. (2) God desires that we do good (1 Thess. 4:3). (3) Good works prepare us for heaven (Heb. 12:14). (4) Good works are a sign of faith (James 2:17, 25). (5) Good works glorify God (Matt. 5:16).

The Church

The Definition of the Church

What is the church? The church is the name given to the spiritual body of believers united in Christ. Christ is its head, and its life is found in the work and ministry of the Holy Spirit (1 Cor. 12:13). Since the church is united by a spiritual bond, it is of course invisible, but it is real nonetheless. Yet since it unites believers who are part of this physical world, its presence is everywhere visible in the world—in the social relationships of believers, in the organization of their assemblies, and in the acts of worship performed by those assemblies.

The church is also universal. The spiritual bond established by the Holy Spirit is not limited by time or space. From the founding of the church by Christ until today, all believers of every age have been members of the church. Moreover, Christ told his disciples, "Where two or three come together in my name, there am I with them" (Matt. 18:20). In other words, the presence of the church is not circumscribed to a particular place. Though it is often identified with a particular location (e.g., the church in Asia), the bond that forms the body of Christ is as strong between continents as it is between individuals in a particular geographical area.

Over the years, much discussion has centered on the extent to which various visible manifestations of the church at specific times and locations can rightly be counted as the church itself. The Bible gives little warrant for identifying the visible church as *the* church, though it does recognize the church in its visible form. It has leaders, lines of authority, and social and spiritual duties to perform. Jesus, in instructing his disciples about resolving conflicts between Christians, presents the visible church as the final court of appeal, "If he refuses to listen even to the church, treat him as you would a pagan or tax collector" (Matt. 18:17). The authority of the church resides in the presence of Christ, not in visible structures.

Is the church the same entity as the kingdom of God? Insofar as God's kingdom is represented by God's presence and agency in the world, the church is the kingdom. If, however, one understands the kingdom of God as the messianic kingdom promised to David in 2 Samuel 7, then the church, at least in its full sense, is not the kingdom. Many theologians, however, view the church as the spiritual equivalent to the messianic kingdom. Others view it as a distinct entity, not linked to the messianic kingdom promised in the Old Testament. That kingdom, they maintain, will be established when Christ returns.

The Church Within Current Theological Systems: Covenant Theology

Covenant theologians define all of God's dealings with humanity in terms of two basic covenants. (A *covenant* is a legal transaction or contract between two or more persons.) The first covenant between God and humanity, called "a covenant of works," was established before the Fall in the Garden of Eden. To receive the benefit of that covenant (that is, eternal life), Adam had to obey God's command not to eat of the Tree of the Knowledge of Good and Evil. But Adam failed and hence was sentenced to death. God's response was one of grace. He did not abandon Adam in his fallen state. Rather, he established another covenant with him—the covenant of grace—through which Adam was given eternal life on the basis of the future work of Christ on the cross. Adam did not choose on his own to obey God and receive a new heart. God, knowing that Christ would pay the price, freely and graciously gave Adam a new heart.

All future descendants of Adam and Eve are in much the same state as their first parents after the Fall. They are dead in their sins until God gives them new life. God's offer of salvation has remained the same, based on Christ's work on the cross. In the past, God administered the covenant of grace to Israel through the Mosaic covenant at Sinai. In the present age, God administers it through the church. That is, the church has replaced Israel as the people of God. The church is the human administration of the kingdom of God in the present age.

In the context of this view, covenant theology must struggle with the question of what to do with the Mosaic Law. Some covenant theologians have argued that the Law was not an original part of the Sinai covenant and thus need not be obeyed within the church. Others, particularly in this century, have argued that much of the Law is no longer valid for the church today. The laws dealing with the priesthood and the tabernacle, for example, have been abolished in Christ's sacrificial death and priesthood. The laws dealing with the everyday affairs of ancient Israel, the civil laws, are not applicable in the church because we do not live in a society ruled by the church. For most covenant theologians, that leaves only the Ten Commandments as laws that Christians must obey. Some covenant theologians today, called theonomists, do hold that the church should attempt to mandate biblical laws within contemporary society. A more moderate form of theonomy insists that only the underlying principles of the biblical law should be applied to contemporary life. Most covenant theologians reject the theonomist's view.

The Church Within Current Theological Systems: Dispensationalism

Dispensationalism takes a different approach from covenant theology. Simply put, dispensationalists believe that God has dealt with humanity in fundamentally distinct ways throughout much of sacred history. They maintain that God always requires faith alone as the basis of human salvation, but the object of faith varies from one time period to another. Central to this way of thinking is the notion that God remains faithful to his promises to the descendants of Abraham, that they will inherit the land of Israel (Gen. 12:2–3) and a blessing in a future messianic kingdom in that land (Gen. 49:10; Isa. 2:2–4). Viewed historically and biblically, dispensationalists maintain that such promises have not yet been fulfilled.

If indeed God still intends to fulfill his promises to the people of Israel, then the church, as the means whereby God presently carries on his work of salvation in the world, has not replaced Israel. Though Israel has been set aside at the present time, God has not abandoned his people. When Christ returns, he will again work through Israel. As Messiah, he will reign over the physical descendants of Abraham in a thousand-year earthly kingdom, centered in Jerusalem. He will be the rightful heir of the throne of David.

This dispensational view of God's promises to Israel obviously affects one's view of the church. The church is not the new kingdom of God, at least not in the sense of the eternal kingdom promised to David in 2 Samuel 7. To be sure, the church is made up of the people of God and, to the extent that God is King over all the world, the church represents God's kingdom. But the church is not the kingdom promised in the Old Testament; that kingdom will only be established at the return of Christ. Instead, the church is the body of Christ, the assembly of believers, the gathering of those who have received the gift of the Holy Spirit. They are called out of the world to worship God and fellowship with him and other believers. As members of a different dispensation than Israel, the church is not under the Mosaic Law.

In recent years, progressive dispensationalists have altered their understanding of the church. They do not view the church as entirely distinct from Israel. In some sense, it has assumed the role and identity of the biblical Israel in its identification with Christ, the reigning Davidic king. Christ reigns today over the Davidic throne, but that throne is still in heaven. Only when he returns to earth will the church give way again to the physical descendant of Abraham.

The Sacraments or Ordinances of the Church

A spiritual bond unites the church to Christ and the members of the church to each other. Like the church, this bond is invisible. Christ has made provisions for the church to visually recognize and acknowledge the reality of its spiritual ties—through sacraments or ordinances. *Sacrament* means "mystery" and thus designates a physical, visible sign of a spiritual mystery. Two central sacraments have been given to the church: baptism and the Lord's Supper.

Considerable debate has centered on the role such sacraments play in the administration of God's grace—that is, what role the sacraments play in obtaining God's grace. To Roman Catholics, baptism and the Lord's Supper are the means by which individuals receive God's grace; salvation comes through participation in them. Protestants, however, have always maintained that the gift of salvation does not come through participating in the sacraments. Rather, the sacraments are given to those who have already received the gift of salvation. Participation in a sacrament signifies a spiritual reality that has already occurred. Many Protestants refer to them as *ordinances* in order to ensure that the nature and role of the sacraments is not seen as a "sacred" rite that carries spiritual weight strictly of its own accord.

Baptism. Baptism is a physical act that symbolizes the purification of the Christian's life that comes through identifying with Christ's death and resurrection. Within the Protestant church, there are two primary modes of baptism, pouring and immersion. The meaning signified most clearly by pouring water over one's head is purification and cleansing. Bodily immersion into the water, on the other hand, signifies the death, burial, and resurrection of Christ. But the most important aspect of baptism is the fact that it signifies a real spiritual event in the life of the Christian, namely, his or her identification in the divine gift of salvation and in the redemption wrought by Christ's death and resurrection.

The Lord's Supper. The meaning of the church's partaking of the bread and wine in communion is explained in the New Testament. It signifies (1 Cor. 11:26) and commemorates (11:24–25) the spiritual bond that relates all Christians to Christ's death. Just as in the Old Testament Passover meal, eating the Passover lamb was a way to express participation in God's salvation in the Exodus (Ex. 12:8), so eating the Lord's Supper expresses participation in the Lord's death and our need for his free gift of salvation.

The Last Things

Death

What happens when we die? Physically, our bodies begin to decompose and return to the basic elements from which they are made, "for dust you are and to dust you will return" (Gen. 3:19). But the Bible also speaks of the human "spirit," which, at death, "returns to God who gave it" (Eccl. 12:7). This process refers to the account of the creation of man in Genesis 2, where God made Adam from the dust of the ground and "breathed into his nostrils the breath of life" (Gen. 2:7). In the same sense Genesis 6:3 speaks of the God-given spirit living in a human being until God removes it. James speaks about the body being dead without the spirit (James 2:26). Thus, theologians speak of death as the separation of body and spirit (or soul).

This raises the question of where and how the human spirit returns to God. The clearest answer to that question comes from Jesus' parable of the rich man and Lazarus (Luke 16:19–31). This is, of course, a parable, but it gives a broad outline of the nature of the world beyond the grave. When Lazarus died, "the angels carried him [away]" (16:22). His human spirit did not float around the body after death, but rather, as with Enoch and Elijah, angels carried it away. The fact that Enoch, Elijah, and Jesus ascended into heaven without dying also suggests that the place where the angels carried Lazarus was a real place. Jesus called this location "Abraham's side" (16:22), because Abraham is the first one who, when he died, is referred to as being "gathered to his people" (Gen. 25:8). Thus all godly people go to be with Abraham. We also learn from this parable that human spirits are conscious, awake, and communicate with each other after death.

Other statements in the Bible support these conclusions. Jesus, for example, said to the thief on the cross, "Today you will be with me in paradise" (Luke 23:43). Peter, James, and John saw Jesus speaking with Moses and Elijah (Mark 9:4). After his death, Samuel came back as a spirit and spoke with Saul (1 Sam. 28:11–19), even complaining about being disturbed (28:15). David was confident that he would see his dead son when he died (2 Sam. 12:23). These texts all suggest that departed spirits do not just vaporize into thin air. They go somewhere—rather, they are taken somewhere by angels. When they get there, they recognize each other and enjoy each other's company. The apostle Paul even speaks of one whom he knows, perhaps himself, who was "caught up to the third heaven" (2 Cor. 12:2), a place he identifies as "paradise" (12:4).

Resurrection

Scripture gives several accounts of dead people being raised to life. Both Elijah (1 Kings 17:17–24) and Elisha (2 Kings 4:18–37) raised a dead boy. Jesus raised a young girl (Matt. 9:18–26) and Lazarus (John 11:38–44). When Jesus died, "the bodies of many holy people who had died were raised to life . . . went into the holy city and appeared to many people" (Matt. 27:52–53). As far as we can tell, in each of these incidents the dead were given their lives back and resumed living. Such "resurrections," though admittedly miraculous and unique, should not be confused with the biblical notion of the future, and final, resurrection.

Scripture repeatedly reports that at the end of the world, God will raise up all the dead. Their physical bodies will be restored and transformed. They will be given immortality and will stand in judgment before God. As early as Job such a hope surfaces. In the midst of his trials, knowing that death would certainly overtake him, Job remained steadfast in his hope of resurrection: "After my [body] has been destroyed, yet in my flesh I will see God" (Job 19:26). He would not merely go to be with God when he died; he would one day actually stand before him "in [his] flesh." The prophet Isaiah proclaimed to Israel that in the last day, "your dead will live; their bodies will rise. You who dwell in the dust, wake up and shout for joy" (Isa. 26:19). Daniel announced that "multitudes who sleep in the dust of the earth will awake: some to everlasting life, others to shame and everlasting contempt" (Dan. 12:2).

When will this resurrection occur? The answer to that question is complex. In the first place, with the resurrection of Jesus the final resurrection has already begun. He is the first of all humanity who are to be raised at the end of history; he is "the firstfruits of those who have fallen asleep" (1 Cor. 15:20). Just as a farmer knows what his crop will be like when he sees the "firstfruits," so in Christ's resurrection we see what our own resurrection will be like. The general resurrection of the dead will occur during the events that accompany Christ's return. The precise details and sequence of the Lord's return can be worked out by a careful study of Scripture, but there is much discussion about how those details fit together. A resurrection of the righteous— those who will receive eternal reward and dwell with Christ forever—will occur immediately with Christ's coming (1 Cor. 15:23; 1 Thess. 4:13–18). What is not clear is the timing of the resurrection of the unrighteous, though it is often assumed they are resurrected at the same time. In Revelation 20:5, the unrighteous are resurrected after a period of one thousand years.

Eternal Life

The resurrection of the dead is the beginning of a new, eternal life—life in fellowship with God and free from the sting of death. Human beings were not created immortal. When God created man and woman, he offered them eternal life if they would trust and obey him (Gen. 2:16–17). They refused God's offer and were barred from the Tree of Life (Gen. 3:22–24). At the end of history, when believers are resurrected, they will be given a new body— a body like the one Christ received at his resurrection (Phil. 3:21). Christ's body was the same one he had while on earth, but it was transformed. It had once been perishable, but it was now imperishable (1 Cor. 15:42) and eternal. Paul calls this a "spiritual body" (15:44) because it is a body made in heaven and thus not subject to death and corruption as are bodies on earth (15:47–54).

How will the righteous spend eternity? The purpose of the resurrection and transformation of the righteous will be to make them fit to dwell with Christ forever. When Christ returns, the dead in Christ will arise to meet him (1 Thess. 4:16) and will receive their immortal bodies (1 Cor. 15:51–54). Those still alive will be transformed (15:51) and go to be with Christ. Thus, the saints of all ages will be transformed into immortal bodies and dwell with the incarnate Christ forever.

Some believe that this resurrection will usher in the eternal state. Others admit that the return of Christ will usher in the eternal state, but believe that the saints, with their transformed bodies, will dwell with the incarnate Christ here on the new heavens and new earth (see Isa. 65:17–25; Rev. 21– 22, which view the new heavens and earth in terms of the physical locality of the Promised Land). A third approach sees the return of Christ and the eternal state separated by one thousand years (Rev. 20:4–5). Christ returns, the righteous are resurrected, and they reign with Christ over the kingdom of David for one thousand years. At the end of that period, the rest of the dead, the unrighteous, are raised (20:5); all are then judged, and the wicked are condemned to eternal destruction (20:11–15). The period of a thousand years is not mentioned in Matthew 25:31–33. Thus some have held that the concept of a thousand-year reign of Christ over the kingdom of David is merely a part of the imagery of Revelation. There is little doubt, however, that Revelation presents an extended reign of Christ on earth before the eternal state begins.

How will the unrighteous spend eternity? The biblical picture of the eternal state of the wicked is one of "eternal punishment" (Matt. 25:46). Their state is contrasted with the "eternal life," which the righteous will enjoy forever in the presence of God (Matt. 25:46; Rom. 2:7).

The Return of Christ

The church has always cherished the hope that the Lord Jesus will return and establish his eternal kingdom. After he ascended to heaven, the angels who appeared to his disciples said, "This same Jesus, who has been taken from you into heaven, will come back in the same way you have seen him go into heaven" (Acts 1:11b). Though many have tried accurately to predict this return, the church has wisely refrained from doing so. Jesus himself warned the disciples, "It is not for you to know the times or dates the Father has set by his own authority" (1:7).

Though the Bible remains silent about when the Lord will return, it has not refrained from speaking about what that return entails. There is a full-orbed understanding about the events of "the last days." So important is the biblical teaching on this subject that we are devoting an entire volume to it in this series (*Bible Prophecy*). Here we will focus on the central event: the return of Christ.

Christ will physically return some day. The biblical picture of his return is built on the imagery of Daniel 7:13–14, where the messianic King comes in the clouds in the sky to establish his kingdom. Christians today understand the return of Christ in at least three broadly different ways. (1) Some believe Christ will come first only for the church in the "rapture." At that time, the dead in Christ will arise, and along with them, those believers still living will be taken into the air to meet Christ (1 Thess. 4:13–18). After the church is removed from the earth, a time of great trouble (called the Great Tribulation) will afflict all who remain. This time is foretold in Daniel 9:24–27 and described in detail in Revelation 6–19. At the end of the Great Tribulation, Christ, accompanied by the church, will return to defeat Satan and establish an earthly kingdom for a thousand years (Rev. 20:4–6). This is called the Millennium. After that will come the Day of Judgment for all humanity, and then the eternal state.

(2) Others believe the church will not be taken out of the world during the Great Tribulation. The "rapture" of the church (1 Thess. 4:17) marks the end of the Great Tribulation rather than the beginning. The church goes to meet Christ on his victorious return to establish his kingdom. They return with him to enjoy his earthly kingdom for a thousand years (Rev. 20:4–6), after which comes a general judgment and the eternal reign of Christ.

(3) Still others believe that Christ's return will mark the final consummation of all earthly history. There will be no literal one-thousand year, earthly reign of Christ. Upon his return, he will create a new heavens and earth. The church will be resurrected and transformed to live with him forever.

The Millennial Kingdom of Christ
in Christian Theology

Christian theology has developed the notion of the kingdom of God primarily in two directions: millennialism and amillennialism. *Millennialists* understand the concept of the kingdom of God in physical, realistic terms. It is a sphere or a realm over which God rules. In Old Testament times it was centered in Jerusalem and extended throughout the regions of the Davidic monarchy. In the future reign of Christ on earth (the Millennium), Jerusalem will again be the center and the kingdom will be worldwide.

Amillennialists, on the other hand, identify the kingdom of God with the realm of the church or with the sphere of the church's influence. For some theologians, the realm of the church is understood in physical terms, so that the spread of the church's influence throughout the world becomes the spread of the kingdom. Others understand the kingdom of God as a spiritual and ethical ideal. To them, it is not so much a place as it is a reign or relationship. It represents the rule of God over the hearts of men and women in the world. When Christians gather together to do God's work, they advance God's kingdom and spread its influence in the lives of others.

In the early centuries of the church, when the church was a small, scattered, struggling group of believers, the concept of the kingdom as a physical realm yet to be established predominated. Christians looked forward to a future earthly rule of Christ. But as the church began to gain in power and influence, the kingdom came to be identified with the earthly church. As might be expected, such an identification sparked an equally strong ethical and spiritual reaction. Thus the kingdom was also identified by many theologians as the spiritual rule of Christ in the hearts of believers. The human soul was viewed as the spiritual Jerusalem, the place where Christ reigned.

In the early medieval church, a partial synthesis of these two views of the kingdom was worked out by Augustine (354–430). This church father viewed the church on earth as the fulfillment of the earthly millennial reign of Christ, though only insofar as Christ reigned in the hearts of its members. The spiritual reign of Christ was thus realized in the earthly realm of the church. Augustine's view has remained a dominate view of the kingdom up to our own day, especially among covenant theologians. The earthly-physical view of the kingdom finds its continuation in the view of modern dispensationalism.

Pre- and Post-Millennialism

Among those who hold to a literal millennial understanding of the kingdom of Christ, considerable debate has surfaced regarding its relationship to the return of Christ. Is Christ to return before (*pre*) or after (*post*) his millennial reign?

One would think that if Christ is to reign physically on earth during the millennial kingdom, he must of necessity return to earth *before* the establishment of that kingdom. That means the return of Christ is a "premillennial" return. This view follows closely the scenario of Revelation 20:4, where John tells us that the thousand-year reign of Christ will be preceeded by a resurrection of all believers. Most, if not all, dispensationalists hold to the premillennial view of our Lord's return. After a short period of seven years, during which God's wrath will be poured out on the world, Christ will return to establish his kingdom on earth for a thousand years.

A characteristic feature of dispensational premillennialism is its view of human society and the modern world. Dispensationalists are not optimistic about the ability of human government and society to establish Christ's kingdom. They await Christ's return to establish his rule in the world. Before that time, life here on earth will get worse and worse. The church's primary task is to save the lost from this evil world. Dispensationalism has thus been marked by a strong compassion for the lost and an intense desire to help those whom society and human government have cast aside. The motive for this mission has largely been the model that Christ himself practiced during his earthly ministry. Dispensationalists have not so much been concerned to save society as to save those whom society has oppressed.

Postmillennialists believe that Christ will return *after* his thousand-year reign on earth. Obviously, if Christ returns after his reign on earth, that reign is not a physical, spatial reign, but a spiritual, ethical one. The church represents Christ's reign on earth, and the resurrection that precedes his reign in Revelation 20:4 refers to the conversion of individual Christians. Moreover, classically at least, postmillennialists believe that two periods of a thousand years are noted in Revelation 20. The first is the time when Satan is bound (20:1–3), the second when Christ reigns victoriously through the church. Historically, most postmillennialists have believed that the first thousand-year period began around the eighth century, when Christianity's power and influence throughout the Western world began to surge; the second thousand years began sometime early in the nineteenth century, when, once again, Christianity's influence swelled enormously through Western imperialism and modern missions. The wars and disintegration of society in the twentieth century, however, has dealt a major blow to the optimism that flourished in the wake of earlier forms of postmillennialism.

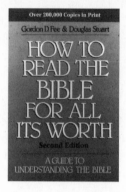
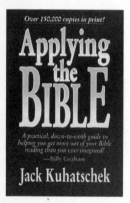

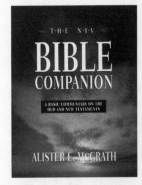

More books by John Sailhamer

The NIV Compact Series

This four-volume series sits handsomely on your desk or bookshelf, ready to answer your Bible study questions quickly and authoritatively. If you read the NIV Bible, then you need this series.

NIV Compact Concordance, by John R. Kohlenberger III and Edward W. Goodrick

0-310-59480-4

NIV Compact Bible Commentary, by John Sailhamer

0-310-51460-6

NIV Compact Nave's Topical Bible, by John R. Kohlenberger III

0-310-40210-7

NIV Compact Dictionary of the Bible, by J. D. Douglas and Merrill C. Tenney

0-310-33180-3

The Pentateuch as Narrative
A Biblical-Theological Commentary

Understand the first five books of the Bible as their author originally intended. Dr. Sailhamer presents the Pentateuch as a coherent whole, revealing historical and literary themes that appear clearly only when it is read this way. A fresh look at the beginnings of the nation of Israel and the earliest foundations of the Christian faith.

Softcover: 0-310-57421-8

Available at your local Christian bookstore.

ZondervanPublishingHouse

Grand Rapids, Michigan

A Division of HarperCollinsPublishers

http://www.zondervan.com